Parenting

A Field Guide

Your Expert Companion From Toddlers To Teens

Parenting
A Field Guide

150 Key Ideas for Raising
Successful, Well-Adjusted
And Confident Kids

Dr. Patricia Nan Anderson

Lake Placid, NY

Parenting: A Field Guide
150 Key Ideas For Raising Successful, Well-Adjusted And Confident Kids

Copyright © 2009, by Patricia Nan Anderson, Ed. D.

Aviva Publishing
2301 Saranac Avenue, Ste. 100
Lake Placid, NY 12946
518-523-1320
www.avivapubs.com

Dr. Patricia Nan Anderson
P.O. Box 1323
Seahurst, WA 98062
www.PatriciaNanAnderson.com
www.ParentingAFieldGuide.com

ISBN: 978-1-890427-55-9

Library of Congress #2008942210

Editor: Tyler Tichelaar
Jacket Design: Growth Industrie Design
Interior Design and Iconography: Growth Industrie Design

Every attempt has been made to properly source all quotations. Internet addresses were accessible at the time this book went to press. Content of referenced websites is solely that of their sponsors and do not necessarily reflect the opinions of the author of this book. Suggestions made in this book are presented as general information and in no way constitute advice for particular situations and challenges.

Printed in the United States of America

First Edition
10 9 8 7 6 5 4 3 2 1

To order additional copies or an audio book version visit:
www.parentingafieldguide.com

This book is dedicated to all parents and
to everyone who has ever spent a sleepless night
worrying about a child.

Praise for
Parenting: A Field Guide

Pure genius! Simply and eloquently written.
Maryann J. Scarborough, M. Ed.

Dr. Anderson sees the hero in the parent. And that makes this book a uniquely valuable resource.
Anne Doczi, M.A., Dinergy Counseling

This book is long overdue and it finally gives parents the tools they need to play a key role in raising their children.
Betsy Stambaugh, Kindergarten Teacher and
Golden Apple Award Finalist

Dr. Anderson's 35 years of experience as an educational psychologist and professor and her experience in the trenches as a parent and grandparent provide wisdom and authenticity.
Flora Morris Brown, Ph.D.,
author of *Color Your Life Happy*

If you want to cut through all the chatter and get to the heart-of-the-matter of raising a grounded, balanced, and self-confident kid, buy this book, read it, and put its wisdom into practice – NOW!"
Donald M. Burrows, author of *Plan While You Still Can*

This book is your go-to resource for the daily challenges of child-rearing.
Brett Clay, author of *Forceful Selling*

Finally, a book well written that covers many of the unknown factors of raising children. This should be mandatory reading for anyone starting a family.
Jim Edmundson, author of *Bullets I've Dodged*

Parenting: A Field Guide provides a healthy, perfectly balanced perspective for parents at any stage.
Geof Kaufman, author of *Mastering Your Choices*

Great information for all parents. Dr. Anderson has figured out the "right" way to approach parenthood.

Brad McColl, author of *Leveraging Your Banker*

Parenting: A Field Guide is a remarkable book and a must-read for all parents who want to raise successful children.

Kate Raidt, author *The Million Dollar Parent*

Dr. Anderson calms a mom's heart and eases a dad's concerns. You'll become a more competent and confident parent with this tool by your side.

Marilyn Schoeman, author of *Speaking Green Light*

When is a parenting guide not just for parents? When it takes a village to raise a child. *Parenting: A Field Guide* is a resource for all caring adults in the village who are committed to raising successful and confident kids.

Val Thomas-Matson, *Look, Listen and Learn*, Commercial Free Children's TV

Thank you Dr. Patricia! This book did not tell me what I was doing wrong, but focused on how I can be the kind of parent I want for my children. Finally, the perfect empowerment guide for anyone who wants to get over the guilt and get on with creating a better human race, one child at a time.

Terri Dunevant, WinCourage LLC

It's all here. Finally a simple yet practical 'how to' book on parenting! Dr Anderson has created a step by step road map to follow to raise happy and successful children.

Patrick Snow, Best-Selling author of *Creating Your Own Destiny*

Every parent wishes their children came with a "how to-book." Dr. Anderson offers just that in *Parenting: A Field Guide,* brilliantly laid out with one idea followed by one practical exercise. If you wish to balance love and limits then start now with this practical parental blueprint.

Debi Waldeck, author of *In The Beginning, There Was Wellness*

Table of Contents

Acknowledgements

Thanks to friends and colleagues whose support has meant everything to me and whose guidance and assistance have carried me to this point. Included among these are Martha Anderson, Susan Balaban, Dr. Paula Jorde Bloom, David Caldwell, Dr. Douglas Clark, Kim Estes, Annika Hipple, Myrna Hoffman, Amy Lang, the late Dr. Marjorie Lee, the late Sr. Grace Pilon, Kate Raidt, Sue Spaeth Riley, Maryann Scarborough, Carol Schiller, Barbara Sher, Elisabeth Stambaugh, Barbara Winter, and Jenny Zappala. This book has benefited from the careful attention of my editor Tyler Tichelaar, the expert direction and continual prodding of my writing coach Patrick Snow, and the great eye and insights of everyone at Growth Industrie Design. Any errors or misstatements that still exist despite their constructive criticism are mine alone, including the omission of friends and colleagues whose names should be here but somehow are not.

Thanks to all of my students past and present and to Sandra Wallace, Harry Hoffman and all the parents at Program for Early Parent Support in Seattle. Thanks to my associates at National-Louis University in Chicago and the inspiration of its founder, Elizabeth Harrison.

Parents learn their craft from their own parents and from their children. I humbly recognize the influence and support of my mom and dad, of my two terrific sons, my wonderful daughters-in-law and my delightful grandchildren. I accept that they may remember events and emotions differently than I have and I beg their indulgence for any disconnects they experience as they read these pages.

Introduction

My first assumption in writing this book is that you don't really need to be told what to do. Unlike other parenting books you might've looked at, this book treats you with respect. It doesn't present the One Right Way To Parent. It doesn't provide you with instructions for some sort of Parenting Make-Over. This book assumes that you can make up your mind on your own, if you've just got some fresh ideas and time to think. I speak from many years of personal and professional experience, but we are both parents, you and I. We're equals.

My second assumption is this: you really care about your kids. You might do things you later regret—we all do—but you want the best for your children. You're willing to think about what's worked for you in the past and what hasn't worked. You're willing to try new ideas and rework your old ones. Because you care about your kids, you're open to finding alternative ways to help them along.

My third assumption is that you don't have a whole lot of time. I don't know any parents who do. So this book is written in short bursts and it's meant to be read that way. Each idea is presented in a single two-page spread, with some thoughts about the topic on the right side and an accompanying exercise or informational bit on the left side. When you want to find out about a particular issue, you can read my ideas on that in under five minutes. Then you can put the book down and think about what you've read as you go about your day. Related topics are arranged in chapters and there's an index for finding things in a hurry.

The fourth assumption is that you and your children are just fine. You might be stressed out. You might have personal troubles of one sort or another. You might be experiencing

Parenting: A Field Guide

some rocky patches. But by and large, you and your children are okay. Not only that but you and your children are full of potential. The possibilities are all there for your family: to share great relationships, to fulfill your potential and to support each other as worthy human beings. I have confidence in you.

And this leads to my fifth and final assumption: that your goal is to raise competent, well-adjusted children who move smoothly and effectively into their adult lives. You love your kids. I love mine. But I'm delighted that my children grew up, moved out of my house, found other people to love and got settled in their own lives. I believe you want that too. Your children will always be your children, but it's great when they go out into the world and bring back to you on their visits home news from their travels and experiences.

So this book is a field guide. It's a manual of thoughts to consider throughout your time as an active parent with kids at home. It's intended to provide you with friendly counsel and pages on which to record your thoughts. I hope you find it useful.

And this book is also a challenge. I challenge you to think more deeply about being a parent than you ever have before and to consider the ideas, strategies, and examples offered in this book as starting points in creating the family experience you truly desire. You can get there. You can realize your vision of well-adjusted, confident and successful kids. This guide will show you the way.

Parenting: A Field Guide

The Parent Vibe
Getting your groove on

A Voice From The Past

Gloria thought she was hearing things. As she got ready to take Hank to the playground she heard someone say, "Don't forget the sunscreen." It was her mother, 2000 miles away in another town but still telling her what to do. Gloria made a face and grabbed the Banana Boat. When would that woman leave her alone?

The answer is "never." You raise your kids the way you were raised, even though you might not want to. You do this even if you think your parents did a terrible job. You do this even if you've vowed to raise your own children differently. When you lose control or when you least expect it, you act as your parents did. Is it any wonder that progress in the human race sometimes seems so slow?

To be a different parent than your own parents you have to figure out what you believe and what kind of people you want your kids to become. Even to be the *same* parent as your parents (hey, you turned out pretty good, didn't you?), you must think hard about childrearing. The pace of life is quicker than when you were a kid. There are more temptations, people are busier, and the pressure to succeed is greater than it used to be—for both you and your kids.

Not only that, but just being a parent is mind-bending. There's a lot to consider and you're not always sure you're doing this right. So give this parenting thing some thought. Do what you can to get into the parenting vibe.

My Idea Of A "Good Parent"

What do you think are the qualities of a good parent? Think of the best parent you know or just imagine what an ideal parent might be like.

_____

_____

_____

_____

_____

_____

_____

_____

_____

_____

_____

_____

_____

_____

If you happen to read fairy tales, you will observe that one idea runs from one end of them to the other—the idea that peace and happiness can only exist on some condition.

—G. K. Chesterton, *All Things Considered*

What Makes A "Good Parent"?

There are all sorts of models for bad parents. Cinderella's wicked stepmother is mean. She's vain and selfish and she loves the stepsisters best. Fairy tale fathers are mindless puppets. They do dumb things like leaving children in a forest where a hungry witch can lure them away.

A child's fantasy parent—a sort of fairy godmother—is not very parental. There are no limits with such a mom or dad and without limits how can a kid know what to do? People who win the lottery and suddenly can buy anything often run into trouble. Being spoiled is never a good thing.

So where is the middle ground between being mean and being permissive? What does a good parent look like?

Psychologist Diana Baumrind says that parenting combines two qualities: warmth and control. The parent who is very warm and lets the kid do whatever she wants is like a fairy godmother. Every child's wish but not good in the long run.

The parent who is cold and really controlling is like the wicked stepmother. There's not much joy there and the parent seems to be the only person who matters.

The parent who is uncaring and lets his children run amok is like the clueless woodcutter in Hansel and Gretel. His kids have to fend for themselves. What's the point of having a parent at all?

The best combination, according to Baumrind, is lots of warmth and plenty of control. Love and limits. This kind of parent doesn't make a very compelling fairy tale, but she makes the happiest, most responsible kids.

Goals Quiz

Find out what you most want for your child. In each row choose ONE of the two choices, even if you don't want either one very much or if you want both almost equally.

I want my child to be...

> **Well-liked** (A) or **Famous** (C)
>
> **A Risk-taker** (B) or **Ambitious** (C)
>
> **Friendly** (A) or **Satisfied** (D)
>
> **Independent** (B) or **Decisive** (D)
>
> **Revolutionary** (B) or **Powerful** (C)
>
> **Accepting** (A) or **Confident** (D)
>
> **Pleasant** (A) or **Visionary** (B)
>
> **Cooperative** (A) or **Forceful** (C)
>
> **Different** (B) or **Hard-working** (D)
>
> **Religious** (A) or **Dominant** (C)
>
> **One-of-a-kind** (B) or **Expressive** (D)
>
> **Imitated** (C) or **Respected** (D)
>
> **Kind** (A) or **Independent** (B)
>
> **Unique** (B) or **Obeyed** (C)
>
> **Admired** (C) or **Imaginative** (D)
>
> **Trusting** (A) or **Moral** (D)

If you have mostly A choices, you are interested in social acceptance for your child. The B choices represent independence, the C choices leadership, and the D choices self-expression.

What do your choices tell you about your values and your expectations?

What Do You Want For Your Child?

A good way to know what you want for your child is to imagine what you *do not* want. You *don't* want your child to be unhealthy, unsuccessful, unliked, unloved, unhappy, or incompetent. That means you *do* want your child to be healthy, successful, likeable, loveable, well-adjusted and capable.

So what? Doesn't every parent?

Even though these things are what all parents want for their children, most parents overlook them. Most parents aim for more specific things. They say, "I want my child to be a computer programmer," or "I want my child to marry someone wealthy," or "I want my child to go to a great school."

It's easier to imagine your kid in a great career than it is to imagine him being capable. The great career is easy to visualize, being capable not so much. And it's easier to imagine how you might help your kid have a great career than it is to figure out how to make him capable. Most of us don't feel all that capable ourselves.

And that's the point. The most important things you can guide your child in becoming are things that seem both ordinary and difficult. It's easier to ignore them. But by the time your kid leaves home at age 18 or 20, you do want her to be ready to go. You want her to be healthy, have a purpose in life, have good friends and maybe even have experienced a significant relationship. You want your child to be emotionally steady and able to do the things adults do.

So it makes sense to focus your parenting on these kinds of goals. Concentrate on the big picture. The nice career and other goodies will come for your kid along the way.

Tips For Feeling More Control

Offer choices between things you can stand

"No, we're not going to go to the zoo today. But we could make cookies or play Monopoly."

"Would you like to pick up your room first or do your homework first?"

Take on the role of the interested but uninvolved observer.

"Isn't it strange that Darren won't eat any vegetables these days? I wonder why that is. Does something happen to a kid's taste buds at age four?"

"I wonder how late Sue would sleep if I let her."

Remember the "Serenity Prayer."

Don't beat yourself up over things you can't change.

God, give us grace to accept with serenity the things that cannot be changed, courage to change the things that should be changed, and the wisdom to distinguish the one from the other.
                                        —attributed to Reinhold Niebuhr

Wanting More Control

One of the biggest surprises of becoming a parent is that you're suddenly not in control of your life as much as you were before. It's astonishing to discover that you really can't control your child. Even though you're the parent, you're not the boss.

A boy I know was a colicky baby who seemed never to sleep. His exhausted parents did everything they could. They were desperate to string together more than three hours of shuteye on any given night. But nothing they did seemed to make any difference. Eventually the child outgrew his colic and learned to fall asleep and sleep well. But those early years were a wake-up call for his mom and dad, in more ways than one. They were put on notice that life with children is negotiated not dictated.

Parents want to be in control for a lot of reasons. It makes life easier, for one thing. It lets you shape your child to match some ideal you have. And it serves as a brace against things that are clearly not controllable, like lightning strikes and drunk drivers. But children don't just go along with what parents want. Kids are people too.

Raising kids is not like conducting an orchestra. Not all the notes and silences are planned in advance. Raising kids is more like being part of a jazz combo. There's a general plan of where the music is going and every musician has his role. But what comes out is often a surprise. No one can tell from the start where the music will really go. Together, the musicians make it up as they go along. And that's the great thing about it.

Get comfortable with uncertainty. Stay flexible. Let your kids play along and you can make beautiful music together.

Ten Things I'm Worried About

When you're feeling less than confident, it helps to write down what you're worried about. Do that here.

1.
   _____

2.
   _____

3.
   _____

4.
   _____

5.
   _____

6.
   _____

7.
   _____

8.
   _____

9.
   _____

10.
   _____

Wanting More Confidence

"I'm afraid of doing the wrong thing."
"I know I won't be a good parent."
"I don't know what to do, so I don't do anything."
"I don't need any help (no one can know I feel anxious)."

Lack of confidence might just be the biggest natural resource problem in our country. But the truth is, it's natural for parents to feel overwhelmed and under-ready. It's okay to feel not-okay about your parenting skills. It's normal.

Nothing quite prepares you for the 24/7 task of being a parent, and the prospect of 18 years of 24/7 is enough to make anyone cringe. But parenting is not so much about doing the right things every moment as it is about thinking the right thoughts and making a good effort. And the right thought is:

"I'm good enough. I can learn on the job and we'll be okay."

Because that's the way it happens. You and your child, working together, learn on the job. You learn how to relate with each other, how to grow together, and how to cooperate in raising each other. You are raising a child but your child is raising a parent. Being open to each new day is all you both need.

When you were a little kid, you thought that adult life was all ATM machines and calling the shots. Now that you are an adult, you know that none of that is true. Being an adult means feeling just the same as that kid you once were but with a whole lot more responsibility.

But you're good enough. You can learn on the job and you'll be okay.

Reliable Online Help For Parents

Here are some organizations that can be trusted to have solid information for you. Be sure also to look for state and local organizations that have support groups and other assistance for parents.

Center for Infant Studies
www.psych.stanford.edu/~babylab/

Children's Defense Fund
www.childrensdefense.org

Future of Children
www.futureofchildren.org

Medline Plus
www.nlm.nih.gov/medlineplus/medlineplus.html

National Association for the Education of Young Children
www.naeyc.org

PBS Parents
www.pbs.org/parents/childdevelopment/

Talaris Institute
www.talaris.org

Tufts University Child and Family Web Guide
www.cfw.tufts.edu/

Zero to Three
www.zerotothree.org

Ask For Help When You Need It

Let's face this straight up. There may be "no such thing as a dumb question" but there are many questions that make us feel dumb if we ask them. People have been making babies for millennia but no one knew at the start how to raise those babies. Every parent is a first-time parent.

You have questions. None of these is a dumb question.

There is not only no such thing as a dumb question but neither is there such thing as a simple answer. Research into the most ordinary things turns up surprising and hotly debated results. There are always more ways of looking at a problem than just the most obvious. Research findings don't always agree with each other.

If not even the experts agree on any particular issue, you can be forgiven for not feeling confident on that issue yourself. But that doesn't mean you can throw up your hands and just do whatever comes to mind. It means the answer is more complicated than Yes or No. Get information and ask for advice.

There are all kinds of resources for you. People are happy to help and are delighted to have you ask. So talk to your friends, your parents, your neighbor, your doctor, your public health nurse, your librarian, and people walking babies in the park. Read books, scope out the Internet and check out magazines. Help is everywhere. Don't be too shy or embarrassed to ask.

Then think about the answers you get. Recognize your new expertise, now that you have all this information. Decide what to do based on what you've learned. Then get ready. Another parent is going to ask you about this. Her question will not be dumb and the answer won't be simple. But you'll know what to say.

Attachment
Feeling like a family

Not Just Attached, Super-Glued

When your baby first came home, I bet you hovered over the little bundle of joy every chance you got. So cute. So amazingly perfect.

After a while the newness wore off and you probably began to feel like you were at the beck and call of a mini tyrant. It seemed as if there were never any time that wasn't dominated by the baby, by feeding him, changing him, bathing him, or trying to put him to sleep. The time he *was* asleep was not long enough to wash all his clothes, get some food for yourself and take a nap. *All* of your sleep came in naps back then, even at night. It was weeks until you got more than a couple hours of rest at one go.

So it seems hard to imagine that attachment with your baby might not happen when the two of you often seem welded together. But the bond between a child and a parent is so key to all the development that comes after that it's worth noticing how attachment happens and what can get in the way.

Notice two things before we start. First, attachment is a two-way street. Not only does the baby become attached to you but you become attached to the baby. And attachment happens with both of a child's parents and even other caregivers, like a daily babysitter or grandparent.

Also, no matter what has happened so far, you can work on improving attachment even now. It's worth the effort.

The Temperament You're Born With

Ever wonder why babies seem to come out of the womb with a personality already there? Psychologists Stella Chess and Alexander Thomas found that babies are born with one of three ways of reacting to the world. These three temperaments are Easy, Slow-to-warm-up, and Difficult.

Everyone loves the Easy child, who is adaptable and is pretty much happy. The Difficult child is fussier and more demanding but also action-oriented. The Slow-to-warm-up child needs time to adjust to unfamiliar people and situations. Chess and Thomas found that about two-thirds of the babies they tested fell into one of these categories (with most of those being Easy babies and the fewest being Difficult). Not only that but these patterns of behavior stick with a person throughout life.

What this means for you is a couple things. First, your child comes with a preset way of behaving that you cannot change. Second, knowing that your child has these preset patterns helps you anticipate his reaction to situations. And, finally, since these patterns last throughout life, *you also* have a basic temperament.

Write down which of the three temperaments you think you might be and why. Think also about your child and his or her temperament.

My temperament is probably:

because:

My child's temperament is probably:

because:

How Your Child Thinks Of You

In the beginning, your child doesn't think of you at all. A newborn is one big ME. Infants can feel rage, disgust, joy, and fear, but none of these, not even rage, is directed at anyone in particular. For the infant, there is no one else. There is just ME.

Gradually, over the next few weeks and months, a baby grows in his ability to notice that he is not alone in the world. He comes to realize that the people who move in and out of his field of vision are always the same. He recognizes Mom and Dad and even enjoys being with them. But he still is completely centered on himself. He is not capable of being bad or mean or even demanding. To be those things he would have to understand that other people are disconnected from him. He can't really realize that.

By the time a child is about 10 months old, he figures out that other people are separate from him. Mom is not just an accessory that is sometimes handy but is actually another person, who can leave and come back. But the baby still doesn't know that Mom has her own agenda and emotions. The baby is still entirely self-centered.

Not until 18 months or even older can a child identify his own feelings and understand that other people have the same feelings too. Not until then can a child learn to be patient (for a little while). And even at that age this understanding is not complete. The child is still self-centered. Mom is still a servant in his eyes.

It takes a very long time before a child can *intentionally* upset his parents. He is incapable of learning that what he does is upsetting, so he is incapable of changing his behavior. Parents have to be patient and forgiving. They have to be ready to wait for a child to see that parents are people too.

What Words Describe Your Child?

Check the words that remind you of your child.
What do you think about your choices?

☐ adorable	☐ different	☐ naughty
☐ agreeable	☐ difficult	☐ nervous
☐ alert	☐ dull	☐ nice
☐ angry	☐ eager	☐ obedient
☐ annoying	☐ easy	☐ perfect
☐ anxious	☐ energetic	☐ plain
☐ arrogant	☐ excited	☐ pleasant
☐ attractive	☐ exuberant	☐ poised
☐ average	☐ fragile	☐ prickly
☐ bad	☐ friendly	☐ scary
☐ beautiful	☐ frightened	☐ selfish
☐ bored	☐ funny	☐ shy
☐ brainy	☐ gentle	☐ sleepy
☐ brave	☐ gifted	☐ smiling
☐ bright	☐ good	☐ splendid
☐ calm	☐ graceful	☐ stormy
☐ careful	☐ grumpy	☐ strange
☐ cautious	☐ happy	☐ stupid
☐ charming	☐ healthy	☐ super
☐ cheerful	☐ helpless	☐ talented
☐ clean	☐ homely	☐ tense
☐ clever	☐ innocent	☐ testy
☐ clumsy	☐ inquisitive	☐ thoughtful
☐ confused	☐ jealous	☐ tough
☐ curious	☐ jittery	☐ ugly
☐ cute	☐ jolly	☐ wild
☐ daring	☐ joyous	☐ witty
☐ defiant	☐ kind	☐ wonderful
☐ delightful	☐ lazy	☐ zany

How You Think Of Your Child

If this were an adult relationship, you'd be out the door by now. What you've got going with your child seems so one-sided. You give and give and give and the kid takes and takes and takes. You love your child and you just want to be loved back. Is that so wrong?

Well, the relationship *is* one-sided. You're on the side with the fully-developed brain and the experience in how to interact with other people. Your young child is on the side where the brain wiring is not even close to complete and where there is absolutely no experience in dealing with people whatsoever. You are the adult. Your child is the child. You're going to have to take the lead here and commit to building your child's ability to interact.

And you do that by example. You model what you want to see, even if your child is just a baby. You interact with your child in the ways you expect she will someday interact with you.

Respectfully. You want your child to recognize that you are a real person, with opinions and feelings so you start right now to treat her the same way.

Attentively. You want your child to listen to you so you must listen to your child. Talk to her, even though she cannot possibly understand you, and wait for her to respond, even if she cannot talk.

Lovingly. You want your child to want to be around you, so express your pleasure in being around your child. Have fun together; just hang out, even when she is small.

Patiently. You want your child to fit you into her life, especially as she gets older. So fit her into yours. Give your child your undivided attention. Stay calm even when it's hard. There is no rush for your child to be grown-up.

Tuning In To Someone Else

Get a set of blocks or something similar and a friend. The friend can be a child but if no child is around, use your partner or another adult. Suggest to your friend that you play with the blocks by taking turns, adding one block at a time. The only rule is that neither of you may tell the other person how to place his block.

Then do that. Build something together by adding blocks one at a time, taking turns, and without telling each other what your objective is or where to place a block. See what happens.

What happens for me whenever I try this is that I get caught up in picking up cues from my friend about where he is going with the construction. I sometimes try to influence his block placement by where I place my block. But mostly I notice that building this way feels quite different from building together from the same plans and quite different from building all by myself. I find that I learn a lot about my friend by playing this way.

Try it and see how it feels.

Dialing In

It used to be that to listen to the radio, you had to rotate the tuning knob carefully to find the best possible signal. The task was to align your radio's receiver with the frequency of the radio waves you wanted to capture.

Helping your child to become securely attached is so much like dialing in a radio station that it's called "attunement." You tune in to your child's signals, trying to match his emotion, his intensity, and his intent. The child with skillfully attuned parents feels understood, even as an infant. The world feels like a safe place with someone who understands him so well and so obviously has his best interests at heart.

Attachment comes in four types and is pretty much established by about 10 months. And it lasts a lifetime. The **securely attached** child is confident of his parents' interest in him and their good will. About half of children are securely attached. Other children have no confidence in their parents and are **avoidantly attached**. Even as infants they feel they can't count on their parents to take good care of them. **Ambivalently attached** children can't make up their minds. They really could be securely attached, but their parents act inconsistently and the baby never knows which parents will show up: the reliable, caring ones or the distracted, distant ones. Children who have been abused may show **disorganized attachment** and already might be on the way to mental illness.

How do you help your child be securely attached? You tune in to your child's thinking and feeling. You serve as a sort of antenna for your child, picking up on his feelings and broadcasting them back. You don't worry that you might spoil your baby by letting your interactions be all about him instead of all about you. In fact, when you're really dialed in you can't spoil him at all.

Becoming A Role Model

Think of the qualities you want to see in your child when he is grown, and decide how you will start today to model those qualities yourself.

I want my child to be...	So I will model that by doing this...

What It Takes

You know by now that being a parent is not about you. It's about your child. Your role is to guide and shape this little person—who already has a personality of her own—while helping her to feel respected, capable, and well-loved. Parenting is not about deciding what your rules are and enforcing them. Parenting is not about your child fitting in to your adult life. Parenting is about developing the potential of the human being who has joined your family.

So your power is creative power. You move the bawling and self-centered baby toward becoming a competent, caring and confident member of society. But the baby is not just a lump of clay that can be shaped any way you like. You have to work with the child's temperament and abilities. Your power lies in being a skillful and sensitive artist.

And your only tool in this creative process is yourself. You don't need toys or electronic gizmos. You just need to model what you want to see in your child. You have to be the person you want your child to be. No child ever learned to be loving by being yelled at. No child ever learned to be hardworking by being ordered about. No child ever learned to be fair and upright by being tricked and manipulated.

The hardest part of being a parent is being better than you have ever been.

Every block of stone has a statue inside it and it is the task of the sculptor to discover it.
—Michelangelo

What Do You Do To Control Your Anger?

We all get mad. It's what you do about it that counts. Try these ideas and then list some others that you think of yourself or hear about from others.

1. Walk away from the situation. If you can, take a walk.
2. Take three deep breaths, inhaling slowly and blowing out slowly through your mouth.
3. Do push-ups.
4. Put on upbeat, lively music or music that is calming. Dance.
5. Sing a song. Some people like hymns or gospel; some people sing the blues. Sing whatever you like.
6. Call someone. Talk to a friend.
7. Give yourself a neck massage.
8. Recite a calming poem or other inspirational writing.
9. Close your eyes and concentrate on slowing your body down.
10. _____
11. _____
12. _____

When anger rises, think of the consequences.
—Confucius

Never, Ever Shake A Baby

Being a parent isn't easy. It's easy to say "be a good role model" but some days that's just hard. Some days it's all a mom or dad can do to just hold it together.

Some days your child will seem unreasonable. She'll cry and fuss and refuse to stop. Nothing you do will make her shut up. She seems like she hates you. Some days you'll be angry with your child. This will happen. It happens to every parent.

And when it does ... walk away. Put the baby down in a safe place and walk away for a minute or two. Let her cry, it's all right. Take a deep breath. Do some stretches. Call a friend. Don't leave the house and don't leave the baby unattended but put her down. No matter what you do, don't shake the baby. When you've got yourself under control, when you can say, "Wow, she's being a little pill today, I wonder what her problem is?"—only then can you pick her up again. Tenderly, gently. She doesn't mean to be upsetting. She is thinking only about her own misery.

But never, ever shake the baby. When an angry parent loses control and shakes a baby, the baby's brain slides inside her skull. This sliding motion slices off the blood vessels at the back of the baby's head. The baby dies immediately or bleeding in the brain causes death in a few hours. Even if the baby doesn't die, the damage caused by the shaking motion is permanent. She will never be the same again. All because you didn't set the baby down. All because you lost control on a bad day that just got much, much worse.

Being a parent isn't easy. You have to be more grown up than you've ever been in your life. Sometimes there's no margin for error. When you're angry with your child is one of those times.

Use Imagination To Create The Future

The days go by without thinking much about them, but every day is a step closer to a milestone your child will reach. Think ahead to major milestones and imagine what you can do to make sure your child reaches and is ready for each of them.

Your child starts kindergarten
What does your child need to be ready? What can you do *now* to help?

Your child starts middle school
What does your child need to be ready? What can you do *now* to help?

Your child starts high school
What does your child need to be ready? What can you do *now* to help?

Your child starts college or trade school
What does your child need to be ready? What can you do *now* to help?

Your child moves out on his or her own
What does your child need to be ready? What can you do *now* to help?

The Securely Attached Child Leaves Home

Some kids grow up and leave home, maintaining a good relationship with their parents. Other kids leave home okay, but they never let their parents back into their lives. Other kids never leave home at all or leave and come back, leave and come back.

How can you have a kid who grows up and leaves home but still comes by for a visit now and then?

One key is to help him develop secure attachment. Securely attached kids have the psychological moxie to stand on their own two feet and the emotional balance to appreciate their parents, warts and all.

Kids whose parents are not so well attuned to their needs and who have trouble feeling respect for their kids are less likely to want to keep up family ties once they've grown up. But these insecurely and ambivalently attached kids also have the most difficulty making strong relationships with people outside the family. They are more likely than securely attached kids to have trouble staying employed or staying married. They may never leave home to begin with or get a real job.

So while attachment forms when children are very small, maintaining or repairing attachment is an important part of parenting throughout childhood and adolescence. Granted, there are events that can undermine secure attachment that are beyond your control, but the more you can be reliable, trustworthy and respectful toward your child the more likely you are to enjoy a pleasant relationship with your kid when he becomes an adult.

Parenting: A Field Guide

Brain Development
The key to everything

Every Child A Genius

Once upon a time, even the most clever philosophers and scientists thought that a person's brain was pre-set and unchangeable. The notion was—not all that long ago, either—that noble folk are noble because they have inherited better brains and common folk are common because they just didn't get decent brains and never could improve things through study or hard work. A person's ability is inherited, according to this old thinking, and locks him into the same social rung that his parents and grandparents and great-grandparents held.

Balderdash.

We now know that while people are born with different brain configurations , the brain you are born with accounts for only about half of your actual abilities. And in fact, what is inherited are really just *potential* abilities. The other half of brain capacity, including the development of whatever potential we were born with, comes from life experience. Good genes only get a person so far. To be really smart or really creative or really successful, a person has to use the brain he has and has to develop his brain even more.

As a parent, there is not much you can do to alter the brain your child is born with. But you can do a whole lot to help him use what he has and develop it further.

Every child can be a genius in his own way.

Fetal Alcohol Syndrome

When expectant mothers drink in early pregnancy, there's a chance the child will develop fetal alcohol syndrome (FAS). Children affected by FAS are different from other kids in many ways but one of the most challenging differences is in the brain. FAS kids have smaller hills and valleys in the gray matter of their brains than do unaffected children and they have much larger gaps, or ventricles. So the brains of FAS children provide them with less thinking capacity than the brains of unaffected kids. It's no surprise that FAS children often have difficulty learning.

Although heavy drinking in early pregnancy is more likely to cause FAS than less drinking, there is no safe "dose" of alcohol. Also, since FAS is caused during the time the brain is in early development—within the first eight weeks of pregnancy—many mothers don't even know they are pregnant yet and may not realize that having a drink is a bad thing to do.

The wise course is not to drink at all if there is a chance of becoming pregnant. Since younger people may engage in binge drinking and in unprotected sex, it's a good idea to warn your adolescents of the risk of FAS.

What's There To Start

Your head is like a bicycle helmet. A bike helmet has a hard outer shell designed to protect the stuff inside. Within the hard shell is a layer of foam and under the foam layer is your head, the whole reason for the helmet in the first place. In your head there is the same organization: hard shell, a layer of gray matter (back to that in a moment), and, deep inside, the really essential parts.

These essential parts are structures that regulate your heart and lungs and other organs. They are needed just to stay alive so they are buried in the deepest part of the head. The gray matter that surrounds it, even though it's the part of the brain we think of as "the brain," is far less important.

The brain's "gray matter," which is like a bicycle helmet's foam layer, is where we do our thinking. It's shaped like a walnut half, with a left and a right side and numerous folds on the surface. It's as if this cortex were made of a flat sheet of fabric that's too large to fit into the skull so it's been scrunched up to make it fit. Not only does the cortex have hills and valleys but there are spaces on the interior side (where the matter is white), as if it really were all wadded up. The size of these gaps and the number and size of the hills and valleys are clues to the amount of thinking material available in a person's brain.

But the cortex is not one single thing either. There is an area for language, one for math, another for physical coordination, and so on. It's possible for a knock on the noggin to block one kind of thinking (say, reading) while not affecting at all an ability that is located at a different spot in the brain. So the cortex is where thinking happens and this is the part that is developed in "brain development."

What Talents Did Your Child Inherit?

What are you good at? What interests you? What do you like to do and where do you like to be? These are clues to what unique pattern of brain cells you have and to what sort of brain your child might have inherited from you.

List the things you're good at or interested in here.

_____

_____

_____

_____

_____

What about the child's other parent? List that person's talents and interests too.

_____

_____

_____

_____

_____

Do you see these in your child?

Preloaded Software

If your head is like a bicycle helmet, then the brain is like a computer. This is no surprise. But this computer comes preloaded with an operating system and software.

The operating system includes neurons ("brain cells") and cells between the neurons called "glial cells." Scientists still aren't completely sure about the purpose of glial cells. But neurons represent thinking potential. When neurons are needed, they connect to each other in a process that is like wiring a circuit. The number of neurons in various parts of the brain represent the thinking potential in each area.

The areas of the brain that are used most make the most connections and those connections become faster with more use. It's like getting continuous software upgrades for the programs you use a lot. A new skill is difficult because your brain has to get out-of-date software into use. The reason a new skill becomes easier with practice is that the connections get stronger.

Your computer probably came loaded with programs you've never used—strange games that clutter things up. Your brain comes loaded with neurons you might not need too, and just as you delete unused programs from your computer, your brain deletes neurons for things you don't need. This process is normal and good—it makes room for the connections you're making between the neurons you do use. But this is why a newborn has more brain cells than an adult. The newborn brain comes with the full package. The adult brain has discarded some stuff.

So, what gets kept is what's used. Experience plays a huge part in determining what sort of brain your child has. This is where you come in as a parent.

Having Less

Methamphetamine (meth) use causes the brain to shrink. Users have over 11% less brain material in certain areas of the cortex and have about an 8% reduction in the parts of the brain where memories are stored. Meth users may have trouble with memory, hallucinations and feelings of paranoia.

Children whose mothers used meth when they were pregnant can have a range of effects. In the most severely affected children who survive past infancy, there can be severe brain damage. This damage can cause long-term difficulty with learning and with physical coordination. There is no "safe dose" of meth for pregnant women.

The effects of meth addiction are devastating for adults and for the children they expose to this drug. In many ways, there is no complete recovery.

Brain injuries and insults of all sorts are often permanent. It's obviously important for parents to do what they can to protect their kids' brains and to avoid behaviors that can damage them.

Getting More

So your brain comes preloaded with neurons inherited from your parents. If your parents were musical or artistic or athletic, you probably inherited more neurons in those areas of your brain. What you inherited can be affected, before birth and after, by toxins and injuries, but basically you are born with the full starter-set.

During the first years of life, the brain decides what neurons it needs to keep. For some activities, like language, there is a deadline by which the neurons need to be used. If the use-by date passes, the neurons for that activity are deleted. Usually you don't need to worry about losing essential stuff. Only if a child is severely neglected or profoundly disabled is it possible for key brain abilities to be unused long enough to disappear completely.

Of more concern is connecting the neurons that are kept. Those neurons represent only *potential* ability. To be of real use, they need to be connected to each other and used often enough that the connections become fast and strong. It's often said that the brain is "plastic," meaning that it molds itself to whatever you need. A child's brain is most plastic up to about age six and again during adolescence. While neurons continue to be connected every time you learn something new for your entire life, early childhood and adolescence are really important for brain development.

So to help your child develop his full brain potential you need to help him use what he has. Everything your child does builds his brain. But the key word here is "does." To build brain potential, your child has to do real things. Just watching or hearing about something is not enough.

10 Brain-Building Things To Do

1. Talk together. Just don't make fun of your child or tell her she's wrong all the time.

2. Go outdoors. See what's there.

3. Tell a story. You can tell about something that happened to you when you were a kid or tell a fairy tale.

4. Show your child how to do a somersault or jumping jacks. Have your child show you something. Take turns; have fun.

5. Play with things you find around the house, like gadgets, empty boxes, and so on. Fix something together.

6. Walk around the neighborhood together and talk about what you see. Take your older child to an ethnic neighborhood and get a snack.

7. Ask your child to follow some directions. The older the child, the more complex the directions.

8. Play games together. Hide and seek is a fine game and you can play it by hiding toys. Board games and card games are great too.

9. Sing and dance. Play your favorite music and sing along and dance together.

10. Read stuff. Stories are fine to read but you can also read the directions on a package or the ingredients list or a bus schedule or signs you see as you walk around together.

How It Happens

When we think of "brain development," we tend to think of developing school skills, like the ability to read or do math. But everything is controlled by the brain. Reading and math, yes, but also the ability to kick a ball, to recognize faces of people you know, to play guitar, to solve problems, to understand someone's feelings, and to plot a strategy. Everything that makes us human, from physical coordination to emotional stability to intellectual skills is located in the brain.

Go back a few pages and see what you wanted for your child. Those qualities and abilities are all controlled by the brain. And the way to develop the brain is through real-life experiences and human interaction.

Remember that the human brain evolved in the deeps of time and evolution is a slow process. It hasn't caught up yet with what modern humans are doing. So brain development happens today in the same way it did for cave dwellers: through direct experience and interaction with real people. Although older children and adults have trained themselves to learn by reading or listening to lectures, we all still learn best by doing and by having the help of someone who already knows.

For your child's brain to develop its potential, he needs to be active in the world, doing real stuff. He needs the support of attuned parents who can be relied on to help.

The good news here is that there's nothing to buy. Cave people learned enough to invent the wheel without ever going to Toys R Us. In fact, there is no toy or gizmo or class or program that your child must have to achieve her full potential.

The bad news is that there's nothing you *can* buy that will do the job for you. You've got to help your child yourself.

Tom Edison's Mom

The inventor of the light bulb, the phonograph and other modern marvels was called "slow" by his first teachers.

The U. S. National Park Service's Edison National Historic Site at West Orange, New Jersey says Edison "went to school only a short time. He did so poorly that his mother, a former teacher, taught her son at home." The young Edison "learned to love reading, a habit he kept for the rest of his life. He also liked to make experiments in the basement."

This was in the second half of the 19th century. Mrs. Edison didn't have fancy electronic gizmos to help her teach young Tom or even electric light to teach him by. Yet she did what she needed to do. Edison later said, "My mother was the making of me. She was so true, so sure of me, and I felt I had someone to live for, someone I must not disappoint."

You can do this too. You too can support and encourage your child, provide opportunities to explore, and support her learning. If Mrs. Edison could do it, you can too.

If we did all the things we are capable of, we would literally astound ourselves.

—Thomas Edison

Simple And Profound

If there is nothing you can buy that will develop your child's brain potential what can you do to help things along? The answer is simple. But it's also so profound that you might need to rethink your idea of childhood.

A child needs a good environment in which to grow. This means not just good food and adequate sleep and hygiene. It also means loving, supporting parents. Kids who are securely attached to attuned parents, who feel safe and who are respected and appreciated are the ones who develop the best.

It takes no money to support your child in this way. It's possible for every parent to give her child love and limits. But if you provide this for your child he will be among the lucky ones. It's not every child who has this simple advantage.

Your child also needs to do real things. He needs to use his senses, to explore things with his own hands, to go places and see people. He needs to be talked with, to have things explained to him, to be listened to. Real experiences in the real world, shared with caring people.

This, too, requires no money. Any parent can provide this, no matter what his financial situation or neighborhood location or personal history. This is easy. But so few parents take the time. They don't think it's important.

Too many parents think they can hire someone to develop their child's brain for them or just buy an electronic teaching toy and that will do the job. Too many parents just don't realize that brain development happens every moment the child is awake, in every experience he has, with everyone he is around. Development happens in small, continuous steps, just by being together and sharing experiences. You can do this.

Autism: Four Things To Watch For

Autism is an uncommon condition that interferes with children's ability to interact with other people. Since interacting with other people is what humans do, autism can create severe problems.

The good news is there are ways to help children with autism to function better. But the key is to start intervention early. Get a professional evaluation if you frequently notice these behaviors in your child:

1. He doesn't respond to his name. By the time a child is six months old or so, he should turn his head when you talk to him.

2. He doesn't look at what you want him to look at. By the time a child is eight months old or so, you should be able to point out a toy or doggie or something and have the child share this experience with you.

3. He doesn't seem to pick up on others' emotions. Most eight- or nine-month-old children will be sad if you're sad and happy when you're happy. If your child seems oblivious to others' feelings, that's a red flag.

4. He doesn't pretend. By the time a child is a year or eighteen months old, she should be able to understand that you're pretending when you hold a banana up to your ear and say "hello?" She should be able to "talk on the phone" with a pretend object by this age.

If you think there's a problem, check it out.

What If There Is A Problem?

Because everything you do originates in the brain, the brain is one place to look if your child has a problem with any developmental stage. And your child's brain is vulnerable to all sorts of injuries and insults, caused by knocks on the noggin, exposure to toxins (like lead), diseases (like German measles), and chromosomal differences (like Down syndrome and autism). In addition, as we've seen, simple neglect and lack of exposure to life experiences also interfere with normal brain development.

But we've also seen that the brain is *plastic*. It responds to new information and can reshape itself in amazing ways. So even when there is a huge problem in the brain, there are ways to work around those.

This means that if you suspect your child is not developing normally or if you suspect your child was exposed to something that might affect her brain, get professional advice. And don't wait until your child starts school. Get help as early as you can. The earlier a problem is identified and a plan to fix it is in place, the more likely there can be real improvement made.

Be persistent. Most pediatricians will take a wait-and-see attitude and often this makes sense. Kids do develop at different rates and yours may just be a late-bloomer. But if you really believe there could be a problem and if you are really concerned, then insist on an evaluation by a specialist. Most locales have early intervention services available that will do screening at little or no cost.

Don't wait. Better to be told "it's nothing" than to be told years from now "you should've got help sooner."

Brain Building Tips

How often does your child engage in these brain-building activities and habits? How often do you?

Your child?   You?

Exercise until out of breath
Get at least 8 hours of sleep
Eat a balanced breakfast
Eat fish, nuts, olive oil, avocado
Solve problems or puzzles
Play board games or card games
Play a musical instrument or sing
Do math
Write
Speak a different language
Teach something to someone
Learn new things
Create art or invent things

How often does your child AVOID these brain-clogging activities and habits? How often do you AVOID them?

Your child?   You?

Eat sugary foods
Do the same things every day
Just do routine things
Dabble in drugs or drink too much
Smoke
Feel full of stress and anxiety

Brain Development Never Stops

At what point does experience no longer matter? When can you stop thinking about the effect on the brain of what your child is exposed to? The answer is you even need to consider the effect of what *you do* on *your own brain*. Brain development never stops.

Myrna Hoffman, award-winning toy developer, showed me her Morph-o-Scope recently. This fascinating toy combines art and physics in a mind-bending exercise of perception and illusion. Trying to get my mind to grasp this (and this is a toy intended for kids from kindergarten on up!) I could almost feel the neurons stretching in response to new information. Brains develop through experiences throughout life.

So do you still need to be concerned about your older child or teenager's brain development? Yes, you do.

As much as you can, make sure your teen gets enough sleep at night—at least eight hours—and nine or ten is better. Sleep is necessary to solidify new memories and learning. Make sure your teenager eats a balanced diet, with enough omega-3 fatty acids (from nuts, fish, and avocado, for instance) because those fatty acids are needed to build the insulating sheath that coats the neural connections.

And provide your teen with opportunities to make decisions and use her ability to see the consequences of her actions. The last brain area to come online is the prefrontal cortex. This area is responsible for our ability to think things through. As we know, life experience is what builds brain ability, so make certain your child has opportunities to make hard decisions. Making decisions is important to brain development.

Learning To Talk
The important first step

As Natural As Breathing

Birds sing because that's what birds do. Humans talk because that's what humans do. You no more need to "teach" a child to talk than a bird "teaches" another bird to sing. As long as the bird is around other birds who sing and as long as a child is around other humans who talk, singing and talking will develop all by themselves.

They're as natural as breathing.

Parents eagerly anticipate a baby's first words not because they're afraid the baby won't learn to speak but because being able to talk is so important to communicating with him. You feel that if you just knew what you're child was thinking, you'd be able to help him better. And that's true. Being able to put thoughts into words is a key step in being a fully-functioning person.

As long as your child hears people talking, he will learn to speak (and for profoundly deaf children, as long as they see people signing to communicate, they will learn to sign). There is nothing special you need to do. But talking and thinking are closely related. And to develop the best thinking, your child needs more than just the minimum of talking. What your child needs is what we'll discuss next.

I learnt most not from those who taught me, but from those who talked with me.

—St. Augustine

Stages In Language Development

We all use gesture and even little babies use gesture to communicate. But oral language develops along these stages.

Preverbal-non purposeful; Birth to about 8 months
The child makes many different sorts of sounds but pretty much randomly and without any thought behind them.

Preverbal-purposeful; about 8 months to 1 year
The child tries to communicate his thoughts by making sounds, sometimes making the first sound of a word, like "buh" to mean "bottle."

Single-word speech; about 1 year to 1 ½ years
The child says one word to communicate entire thoughts, like saying "dog" to mean "look, Mom, there's a dog." The child knows about 50 words by 1 ½ years.

Two-word sentences; about 1 ½ years to 2 years
Two words are combined to make a sentence, like "Get more." Often only Mom and Dad understand the child.

Three-word sentences; about 2 to 3 years
The child assembles short sentences. By age three, the child can be understood by people outside the family and he knows about 1,000 words.

Complex sentences; about 3 to 5 years
The child speaks in sentences that are more and more like adult speech. By age 5, the child knows 2,000 to 5,000 words.

The Amazing Trick

Your baby had nearly fully-developed hearing even in the last few months before birth. He was eavesdropping on your conversations even in the womb. Learning language is that important: the hardware to hear is ready to go from the first moments of life.

So why does it take nearly two years for your child really to start to talk? Is there any reason to pay attention to a baby's language much before that?

Actually, a lot happens for language development in the first few months of life. Babies hear what is spoken around them and their brains shape themselves to be receptive to only the speech sounds spoken by people around them. By about 10 months, babies who once could hear any speech sound of any language in the world have narrowed their focus to only the speech sounds of the language spoken at home.

Babies practice those speech sounds. They babble. They babble in what sound like sentences. They seem to be trying to communicate, long before they can actually speak.

Slowly, your baby refines his babbling to imitate the words you emphasize. By about 11 months, your child says his first word, even though your friends couldn't quite hear it. More words quickly follow and pretty soon other people believe that your kid is talking. Yay!

And then, *if you talk to your child*, the "language explosion" takes over. By the time your child is five he will have learned over 5000 words and will be able to speak in full sentences, ask questions, talk about yesterday and tomorrow, and even lie once in a while. This happens pretty much by itself. Your child is pre-programmed to learn to talk. It just happens.

Look Who's Talking Quiz

Pay attention for an afternoon or a day to what you say to
your child, how much you talk, and how much she talks to
you. See what you find out. Then answer this quiz.

I'm likely to talk about:
☐ A toy my child is playing with
☐ The work I'm doing
☐ The birds outside the window

I usually:
☐ Ask questions
☐ Give orders
☐ Make conversation

I do the talking:
☐ Almost all of the time
☐ About half of the time (my child talks the other half)
☐ Almost none of the time

When I talk my child:
☐ Usually talks with me
☐ Sometimes talks with me
☐ Usually ignores what I say

My child mostly talks about:
☐ What he's doing right then
☐ What I'm doing right then
☐ Things he knows or wants to know about

My child usually:
☐ Asks questions
☐ Gives orders and demands
☐ Makes conversation

Your Role

So if kids learn to talk pretty much on their own, what's your role? Do parents matter?

Absolutely. In fact, you're the most important part of the puzzle. Without you, your child would have had *the potential* to speak but never really got there. Those 5,000 words by age five? Those come from you.

But the 5,000 words don't come as vocabulary lessons. Teaching a child to talk is not like cramming for the SAT. The 5,000 words come in everyday conversations together, talking about the weather and what you did today and what's for dinner.

Your role is to model language. You talk with your child as if she were a friend. You ask about her day, talk about what clothes she wants to wear and so on. You ask questions and wait for the answers. When you talk to your child, you don't just give orders. You don't just speak in as few words as possible. You demonstrate how people talk.

Children who start kindergarten differ on how many words they know and on how they put together sentences. Kids who do better in school know more words and know how to say what they want to say in a way that others can understand. They have had practice with a good role model. Kids who do less well in school know fewer words and have trouble arranging those words into meaningful sentences. What practice they've had with speaking has been limited to talking with other kids and to replying to an adult in as few words as possible. For some kids, their only consistent model for speech is the television, which provides only a one-way interaction.

To learn language, children have to *hear* language and they have to have *practice* speaking it. That's what you're there for.

Word Play

Stuck in traffic? Waiting for the bus? Here are word games to play with your child that will build vocabulary

Opposites. One person says a word and the other person replies with its opposite. This is fun enough with young children and words like "up," "fast", and "loud." But try it too with your older kid and harder words like "complicated," "obvious," and "local." Take turns.

Analogies. One person starts an analogy and the other person finishes it. So you might say, "As big as a..." and your child might finish the analogy with "skyscraper." You can then switch roles or you can simply continue to make more and better analogies for the original idea.

Synonyms. You and your child think of as many words as you can that mean the same, or about the same, as another word. So maybe you start with the word "big" and between you, you come up with "large," "huge," "enormous," "massive," and so on.

Alphabet Chain. You and your elementary age or older child try to create a 26-word sentence or short story that uses words that start with every letter of the alphabet in alphabetical order. "A big cat dumped eggs for ..." See how far you can get. Or...think of words to fit a category that begin with each letter of the alphabet, in order. For example, *animals*, starting with "anteater, bear, cougar, dinosaur, elephant," and so on.

More Is More

Be extravagant. Use lots of words, use complicated sentences, say silly things. The more you use language with your child the smarter he will get. As long as you let your child talk too, more language from you means more language for him.

Talk about everything. Ask questions. Explain things. Make your conversations pleasant and treat your kid with respect. Talk to him as if he were a friend.

Sing. Singing is a great way to learn new words and figure out what something means. Song lyrics are not always direct. A person has to figure out what the song-writer meant by a particular phrase. This is all part of learning a language. Not only that, but singing is fun.

Recite nursery rhymes, slogans, and famous phrases. Poets use language in odd ways and that makes a person stop and think about what is meant. Rhymes and slogans are fun to say and they sometimes have new words in them.

Play with words. When you're riding on the bus, play a game together like thinking of all the words you can that start with B. Or words that mean where something can be put (like "on," "under," and "near"). Or words that could describe a gorilla.

Tell stories. Tell what happened today. Ask your child what happened at child care or at school. Make up a story where you each stop right at a critical point for the other person to add more.

When it comes to language, more is more.

"You Know What?"

Conversation with my five-year-old grandson usually is peppered with the words, "You know what?" It's like the set-up to a knock-knock joke. He says, "You know what?" and I say, "Tell me what."

This gets me a single sentence of information. Last night it was:

"You know what?"
"Tell me what."
"Spiders have two parts to their bodies: the head and the abdomen."

I then said something like "really?" and he said again, after the pause of a half second:

"You know what?"

"Tell me what."

This process often seems like it could be speeded up quite a bit, but I accept that this is how his mind thinks right now, in single bits of information, and to keep the conversational ball rolling, I have to play along.

Do what you need to do to keep the conversational ball rolling in your house, whether your kid is 5 months old, five years old, or fifteen. Play along. You just may learn something about spiders, and you'll surely learn things about your kid.

Best of all, your kid will learn to talk and talk well.

Conversation Is Key

It's easy to get impatient. You're busy, you don't have much time. If you wait for your kid to tell you something you'll never get anywhere. But if you don't wait, you're *kid* will never get anywhere. You've got to slow down and take the time to talk. And to listen.

Think of something you learned that required some practice but is now automatic. Maybe you learned to drive a car or ride a bicycle or make pancakes. The first few tries were probably not all that successful. Even after you mastered the techniques, you had to be careful to remember all the steps. You had to think about it. You were slow.

But you learned. You got faster with practice. Now you hardly need to think. But if someone had taken over—because you were so slow—and done things for you, you would never have learned. You might even have felt that the job was too hard for you. It might've seemed easier just to let someone else do it.

You want your child to learn to talk, and not only that, you want your child to learn to talk *well*. You want him to be able to put his thoughts into words and to think new thoughts because he has the language to do that. And learning this takes practice. It takes time to master.

Speaking might be natural, but it still takes time to get really good. So talk with your child and listen. Give him the time he needs to put his thoughts into words. Be patient.

A conversation is a dialogue, not a monologue.
—American writer Truman Capote

Nine Tips For Talking To Teens

You wait for your child to learn to talk; then she talks your ear off, and then, when she hits the teen years, she clams up. How can you keep your kid talking to you?

1. Ask questions that can't be answered with a single word or just by "yes" or "no."

2. Ask her opinion about something (and don't argue about what she tells you).

3. Ask for help in solving a problem.

4. If you get no answer, answer your own question, as if talking to yourself, and leave a space for your child to chime in.

5. Avoid asking personal questions or personal questions about her friends.

6. Avoid saying anything about her refusal to talk or your frustration with this or how hard you're trying. If you don't get a response when you talk, let it go and try again another time.

7. Try striking up a conversation when you're both in the car or doing something together. Keep it natural and casual.

8. Speak slowly and quietly. Don't shout or rush things. Use short sentences and leave spaces so your kid can also talk.

9. Smile. Be pleasant no matter what.

How Long Do You Wait?

What if your child doesn't talk at all? When is a late-talker a problem?

If your baby doesn't babble by six months, then talk to your doctor. If your baby doesn't seem to be trying to make words by fifteen months or so, then have her checked out. And if your child isn't talking, or can't be understood by anyone but you, by three or four years old, then that's a concern.

While certainly there is a range for learning to speak and your child may be within normal limits, if you think there is a problem, ask. The earlier you get help the sooner your child can make progress.

There could be several things going on. Your child may not have had opportunities to use language, because his older sister always speaks for the two of them, or no one ever talks much with this child. He might just need practice.

Your child might be very shy or timid. There may have been some traumatic event in her life that she expresses by not talking. She might need help with that.

Your child might be able to understand language perfectly but have difficulty making the correct sounds. Or, your child could have a hearing problem and not be able to tell the difference between some sounds.

Or there could be a problem like autism that makes language seem less important to your child or makes it impossible for her to learn it easily.

There is help available for all of these problems, often at no cost. So wait a while, but not too long.

It's All Relative

When I was a kid, my mother wouldn't let us say the word "fool" because she said it was forbidden in the Bible. I never bothered to find out whether that was true but I was pretty careful to use that word only out of her earshot.

What words were forbidden by your parents? If you dare, write them here:

How frequently or easily do you say those words today?

What words do you or will you forbid your children to say? Write them or describe them here.

Are those words the same ones forbidden to you?

What concerns you most about bad language and your child? How can you solve the problems you're having with bad language or that you foresee for the future?

Kids Say What They Hear

Mom and Dad were concerned about Randy, the youngest of their kids. He was four and had never really talked. Granted his older brothers and sisters seemed to know what he wanted all the time and Randy was pretty spoiled. But four! When would he ever speak?

Then one day, Randy was refused a treat. He was furious. Everyone knew just how furious when Randy said, "Then you can keep your @#*&!% cookie!" Yipes! Not the "first words" Mom and Dad were waiting for.

If you want your kid to swear like a sailor, then model that. Your child will talk the way he hears you talk, so watch your mouth! Bad words and slang are cute for a few seconds. Then you realize your kid doesn't understand that there's a time and place for such language. He can't tell whether it is that time and place or not. You've not only created a kid who can make you cringe but you've also set your child up for disapproval from others through no fault of his own. He has no intention to shock and offend. He's just doing what's been modeled for him.

So cut your kid a break. Be careful of your speech and enforce decent language in your friends when your child is around. The saying about there being a time and place for everything applies to you too: when you are out with friends it's one thing, but when you're around your child, that's another.

As your child gets older, he will naturally try out language he thinks makes him seem older and more sophisticated. Your role is to remind him of the "time and place" rule and to enforce the fact that your home is never the place and conversation with family members is never the time for profanity and vulgarity. Model what you want to hear and insist that your child follow your lead.

Talents Come In All Varieties

What special talents would you like to encourage in your child? What are your child's natural interests?

☐ Fluent speaker of several languages

☐ Fine artist in drawing, painting, sculpture or ceramics

☐ Exceptional athlete

☐ Respected spiritual leader or ethical guide

☐ Sought-after connector between people

☐ Super public speaker and motivator

☐ Wonderful musician, composer or singer

☐ Creative problem solver

☐ Widely-read author, poet or commentator

☐ Clever programmer, inventor or scientist

☐ Intuitive interpreter of animals and the natural world

☐ Gifted actor, entertainer or performer

☐ Brave adventurer, explorer or mariner

☐ Other _____

☐ I'm waiting to see my child unfold

☐ I'm waiting to see what my child chooses

☐ I'm willing to support my child in whatever she decides

Decisions that are made about what will be accessible to children help shape the kind of minds they will come to own.
— Educational philosopher Elliot Eisner

Learning Another Language

Knowing more than one language is a good thing, right? So what is the best age to learn another one?

If you're like lots of people, you struggled to learn a second language in high school with mixed results. Compared to the ease with which little kids learn their home languages (pretty close to perfect in four years or less) learning a language as a teenager doesn't seem very effective.

And it's not. The best time to learn any language is when a person is very young.

So if you have the opportunity, enroll your child in a language-immersion elementary school and keep her enrolled there. Even better is to have your Hungarian grandmother come by frequently to speak Hungarian with your baby. Babies who are exposed on a daily basis to a native speaker of a second language will learn both that language and her home language (though both a bit more slowly than if they were learning only one language).

If your child must learn a language after about age 11 then language immersion is the best way to go. A trip to France or a new life in the Philippines will make learning French or Tagalog as quick as it can be. Not easy and not comfortable, but quicker than any other way.

As with everything else, the most effective way to learn a new language is through real-life experience and in the presence of other people. If you can provide that for your child, fine. If you can't, concentrate on developing his abilities in other areas.

Child Care
Who can take your place?

Going Back To Work

Carlotta knew exactly how this was going to play out. She would work right up to the day of her delivery then take her full 12 weeks of maternity leave and then go back to work full-time. She would take the baby to her mom's during the day. Carlotta needed the money and, more importantly, the health benefits. But after R.J. was born, she started to feel differently. How could she leave him with anyone? Carlotta didn't want to be away from her baby at all.

Karen decided long ago that she would stay home after her baby was born. The family would miss the second income but Karen and her partner were convinced the sacrifice would be worth it. But Paolo was not even four months old before staying home got old. Karen felt like her brain was melting and she missed her old work pals. She wondered whether she was a bad mother for wanting to put her son in child care and go back to work.

There was a time when women had no choice. They gave birth one day and milked the cows or hoed the garden the next. More privileged women had little choice either: society required that they find a wet-nurse to care for their babies so they could continue their social lives unencumbered by infant demands. Today we have choices, though that doesn't seem to make the decision any easier.

When it comes time to consider day care for your child, what do you do? And what does it mean if you change your mind?

Child Care Options Worksheet

Do some research and keep notes here of what you find.

Child care centers you might use:

Family child care homes you might use:

What you find out about nannies:

Relatives you might be able to use:

Options for after school care:

Time Matters

When you try to think about child care, time matters. As Carlotta's and Karen's experiences demonstrate, what you think you want to do might be different from your later feelings on the matter. You might change your mind. And that's okay.

It's not really possible to know in advance how you will react to the birth of your child, even the birth of a second or third child. Before the baby is born, we have the silly notion that the world will continue on after the birth just as it did before, the only change being a new person in the family. But, of course, a new person in the family changes everything. All the dynamics and routines are thrown off by the new arrival. Your life becomes different in ways you couldn't have anticipated.

So the first thing to do in considering child care is to stay flexible. It makes sense to have several different plans sketched out, so you have an idea of how to act under a few different scenarios. Get an idea of how your mother-in-law feels about watching the baby for you. Check out a few child care centers and family child care homes and even put your name on a few waiting lists. See what it costs to have a nanny and really think about how you will feel about having a stranger in your home. Play with the costs and see what you can afford.

But don't mentally or financially commit too early to one plan or the other if you can help it. Give yourself some leeway and let things evolve.

Timing matters too. Putting your child in daycare at age four is a whole lot different from putting him in daycare at age six weeks. We'll look at that next.

You're The Center Of Your Baby's World

Fact: Babies hear their parents' voices even before they are born and they can recognize your voice immediately after birth.

Fact: Babies as young as three days recognize their mothers by smell (and mothers also can recognize their babies by smell even though they might not be aware of doing it).

Fact: Babies as young as six weeks recognize their mothers on sight and express excitement to see them. Even fathers and other family members are recognized.

Fact: Babies as young as six months can become depressed when they are separated too long from their families. Depressed babies don't gain weight and are slow to learn.

How Early Is Too Early?

Child care centers do not accept babies younger than six weeks. Does that mean that it's okay to place your baby in child care at age six weeks?

Well, what is meant by "okay"? Okay means "acceptable" but it doesn't mean "ideal." In an ideal situation your baby spends his time during the day with an attentive, caring and intellectually stimulating adult, and with the same adult every day.

Certainly, this ideal situation can happen at home with loving and attentive parents who are not stressed financially, have many social supports, and are content with being full-time caregivers to their children. If this describes you and your situation, then do stay home with your baby. Babies do not *need* child care. Your child will not miss anything (at least not until age three or four, when children benefit from some sort of group situation away from home).

But in most families today, the ideal situation combines parental care with care outside the home. Some families need two incomes to get by. For many parents, being home alone with an infant is socially isolating, especially in neighborhoods where no one else is staying home. And for some parents, being home all day makes them crazy. They just can't handle the caregiving role on a full-time basis. The ideal situation is found in a stable child care environment, where a caregiver can provide the developmental support a baby needs.

But back to the six weeks. The longer you can keep your infant home with you, the better. Six weeks is okay, but 10 weeks is better and 12 weeks is better still. The older your infant is, the more established are feeding routines and the bond between you. Six weeks is okay but not ideal.

What It Costs

Figures compiled by The National Association of Child Care Resource and Referral Agencies demonstrate that child care is a major expense.

Child Care Center Costs in 2008

	Infant care	Care for 4-year-olds	School-age care
Highest annual cost per state	$13,437 in New York	$10,524 in Wisconsin	$8,600 in Minnesota
Lowest annual cost and state	$4,542 in Mississippi	$3380 in Mississippi	$2,500 in South Carolina
% of average one-wage-earner household income	57.2% in New York	45.0% in Wisconsin	Not available
% of average two-wage-earner household income	17.3% in New York	14.6% in Wisconsin	11.1% in Minnesota

Even care for the lowest-cost age group in the lowest-cost state still runs over $200 a month. Child care for a single infant can cost more than $1,000 a month. Costs increase, of course, for families with more than one child.

Who's Taking Your Place?

With good, convenient and affordable child care so hard to find, it's tempting to skip some steps in the selection process. But it pays not to jump at the first placement you see. Remember that your child will be spending a lot of time in whatever site you select and with whatever people are there. Take your time. Look around.

Most child care centers ask that you and your child come in for a visit, to check each other out. In fact, avoid any center that doesn't require you to do that. And then take a good hard look. Is the office neat or messy? Are the bathrooms clean? Is there outdoor space and is it safe? If there is a television in every room, ask why that is. Children shouldn't spend a lot of time watching TV.

What licenses does the site or caregiver hold and are they current? If the person is not licensed, what other training or experience does she have that makes her qualified? Ask for references and call more than one of them. When you visit, try to separate out how much you need this child care location to work from your honest evaluation of how good it is.

This kind of careful thinking should go into a decision to hire a nanny too, or even to leave your kid with your sister or your mom. Just because a relative is available doesn't make that person qualified to care for your child. And a nanny whom you don't know will be all alone with your child, without anyone else around to give her a break or keep an eye on her behavior. Check and double-check anyone you decide to hire and really think hard about using a relative. It's more difficult to "fire" your Aunt Cleo than it is to fire a stranger.

Child Care Checklist

What should you look for in choosing care for a child of any age? Here are factors that are associated with high quality care.

☐ **Low child/teacher ratio** (lower than 4/1 for infants, 16/1 for three-year-olds, and 28/1 for school age kids)

☐ **High teacher qualifications** (Bachelor's degree or higher in a field related to children's care)

☐ **Certified teachers** (teaching certificate or child care certificate)

☐ **Low teacher turnover**

☐ **An open-door policy for parents** (parents are welcome to drop in any time)

☐ **Fully licensed by the state**

☐ **Accredited by a national professional organization**

The Importance Of Paying Attention

Child care is one service that's purchased by someone who doesn't actually use it and can't really tell if it's any good. And the person who does use it (the child) is often not able to speak or, if she can speak, is not savvy enough to be able to tell if this is good child care or not. So moms and dads tend to choose childcare for the wrong reasons—price, location, fancy decorations, classy-sounding programs—and then tend to be satisfied with their choice regardless of how bad it really is. Since you won't be using child care yourself, it's important that you think like a child when picking it out. And it's important that you keep an eye on things even after you've made your choice.

If your child could talk and was able to evaluate his needs, he would say that he needs a stable, attentive, and friendly caregiver who lets him interact and be active and who talks to him a lot. He needs a place that is safe and clean and comfortable. He needs intellectual stimulation but no pressure to grow up too soon.

It might be that your child's ideal caregiver is a family member or a nanny or someone at a child care center. But just because a family member volunteers doesn't make that person ideal. Just because all your friends use a particular center or your best friend wants to share a particular nanny doesn't mean that center or that nanny is the best for your kid. Cost and convenience often drive child care decisions when what should drive them is the quality of care and attention your child receives.

And if you make a choice, and then you suspect things aren't going well, don't hesitate to switch caregivers. While having a stable, consistent caregiver is best, a consistently thoughtless, dangerous, or unpleasant caregiver is terrible to inflict on your child. Choose wisely and check often to be sure you made the right choice.

Two Experts Think Outside The Box

Barbara Winter, author of *Making a Living Without a Job*, has helped many people, parents included, find creative ways to earn a living while doing what they most love. For you that might be "while staying home with the kids."

Winter says, "Most people fail to go after their dreams or leave their comfort zones because they haven't taken the time to really think about what rewards their ultimate success would bring them." She recommends studying what other entrepreneurs have done, getting a support system in place, and having the courage to make your dreams a reality. She writes, "Courage is not the absence of fear but, rather, the determination to act because the rewards are worth it."

Life/Work balance expert Kate Raidt, author of *The Million Dollar Parent* agrees. She suggests that you think outside the box in weighing your child care options.

"Ask your employer for what you want," Raidt says. "You might be surprised that you get it." Employers want to keep good employees and they can be more flexible than you might imagine in agreeing to shortened hours, work-from-home arrangements and job sharing.

If the kind of work you do can't be done on a different schedule, Raidt suggests finding ways to do what you do in your own home-based business. Raidt says, "You've got to be creative. People are so used to regular sorts of jobs that they have trouble thinking of new ways to make money. But others have done it."

Weighing Your Options

Child care is expensive and mediocre child care is not much cheaper than quality child care. Faced with high costs, many families get creative.

Figure out if your income will cover the cost of child care at all. Infant care, especially, is so expensive that many parents find that it takes all the money they make by going back to work.

See if you can downsize household expenses so your family can make it on one income. Or see if there's a way to supplement the household income without leaving the kids by running an at-home business. Direct sales (think Avon for instance) is a time-honored way to launch a business from home.

Watching other people's children is another way to stay home with your own kids. If you decide to try this route, be serious about it. Get the proper licensing and protect yourself legally. Remember that child care is a business: be businesslike.

Fewer hours of child care can be less expensive than full time, so you might consider working part time or working overlapping schedules with your partner. But many centers charge full price for less than full-time care if there is not another part-time client to fill up the slot.

Free child care with a relative is delightful when it works out but a nightmare when it doesn't. So think hard about this before you agree and set a date to review together how this is working for everyone.

One of the key things about child care is that just when you think you've got it set, things change. Stay flexible but choose quality.

20 Ways To Enjoy Quality Time

If quality time = comfort, here are some ways to fill in the equation.

1. Sit together with your child and just talk.
2. When you come home, put on soft slippers.
3. Keep a favorite blanket or quilt in the family room.
4. Give or receive a shoulder rub.
5. Peel an orange and enjoy the fragrance.
6. Read together books you enjoy.
7. You and your child take turns singing songs to each other.
8. Let your child take a bubble bath.
9. Warm a cookie in the microwave and eat it slowly.
10. Turn the lights down to a cozy glow.
11. Keep the lights off and watch the night creep in.
12. Have soup for dinner. Even canned soup will do.
13. Take a slow walk in the dark and look at the stars.
14. You and your child ask each other about the day and really listen.
15. Speak in a quiet voice.
16. Pet the dog or cat.
17. Tell stories about when you were little.
18. Have a glass of warmed milk and crackers.
19. Listen to soft, pretty music.
20. Take turns saying nice things about each other.

Quality Time

When middle class families started using child care in earnest, back in the late 1970's and 80's, because more mothers of preschool kids went back to work, there was a lot of talk about "quality time." The idea was that it doesn't matter how many minutes you spend with your children. What matters is the quality of the interactions you have when you're around them.

And quality does count. If you can be attentive and warmly supportive of your child in the hours after you pick her up from child care and before she goes to bed (and over breakfast and on the commute to the center each morning), you will feel connected to your child and your child will feel connected to you. There is no evidence that child care is detrimental to kids' development as long as they feel loved at home.

The trick, of course, is being attentive and warmly supportive after a long hard day of work and with a child who is tired and fussy herself. There's no getting around the fact that both of you are at your best in the middle of the day, when you're apart. The ends of the day are not when we're usually our most charming.

So try hard to make time shared be of good quality. Be as organized as you can be, so that things aren't stressful in the morning. Have a routine in the evening, so that dinner is made, stories read, and baths taken in a predictable way. Avoid mindless entertainment but focus on folding laundry together, playing games, or reading stories. Try to leave a little energy for your child so you can be calm if he is frazzled and difficult.

Working full time (and going to child care full time) is physically and mentally exhausting. We all need some comfort at the end of the day. Comfort is "quality time."

Tips For Parents Of Kids Home Alone

1. Post the phone number where you will be.

2. Designate healthful snacks.

3. Agree on chores or homework to be done.

4. Put parental controls on the TV and computer.

5. Establish rules about who can come inside.

6. Establish rules about where your child may go.

7. Have games, hobbies or other activities available.

8. Make certain that weapons, alcoholic beverages, prescription meds and substances that can be inhaled are under lock and key.

9. Never underestimate the curiosity of healthy children.

10. Call home at least once while you're gone.

11. Let your kids know that you're proud of how responsible they are.

12. Make kids' time alone as short as you can.

13. Do not leave a child younger than 10 home alone at all.

Before And After School Care

All that we've said about child care for preschoolers is the same for elementary school kids using before- and after-school care. It's hard enough going to school for six hours a day. Adding on another hour before school starts and an hour or two after school is over can make for an exhausted and crabby kid. That's not to say you should avoid before- and after-school care. If you need it, use it. But recognize that there will be need for some quality time at home in the evening.

Since before- and after-school care is usually provided on-site at the school, there may be little to choose from in selecting care. But if you can influence the program, try for well-supervised active play, time to complete homework with some assistance, and a warm and supportive staff. If you use a nanny or neighborhood care instead, look for the same things. You want to come home to a child who's had some of the bounces worked out, who's got her homework pretty much done, and who feels happy and well-attended to.

Care in the summer and during school vacations calls for some thinking ahead. Again, look especially for careful supervision and clear expectations for good behavior. Look for a balance of activities. Even a specialty camp should have opportunities for exercise, quiet time, and friendships. Beware of leaving your child home by himself all day.

This is expensive, I know. Twenty years ago as a working single mom, my two sons spent summers on their own. They rode their bikes a mile to the municipal pool every morning, swam an hour for the swim team, then rode a mile back home again (uphill). Exhausted—and basically good boys— they managed fine together. Would I do this today? Probably not. Times have changed.

"But Everybody Else Can!"

Your preteen or teenage child thinks you're the meanest, most restrictive parent on the block. Are you? Or are other parents also trying to hold the line?

Find out. Call around and ask other moms and dads. Talk to them as you stand on the sidelines at a basketball game. Talk to the assistant principal or dean at your child's school.

You might find that you're mired in the Victorian age. If that's the case, you can consider if you want to lighten up or not. But probably you'll discover that "everybody" includes very few kids indeed.

Write down what you find out here.

When I was a boy of fourteen, my father was so ignorant I could hardly stand to have the old man around. But when I got to be twenty-one, I was astonished at how much the old man had learned in seven years.

—attributed to Mark Twain

The Need For Supervision Continues

The older your child the *more supervision* she may seem to need. Your sixteen-year-old is capable of getting into more and bigger trouble than most nine-year-olds, as many parents who've left their teen alone for a weekend found out. Remember that the brain region responsible for seeing consequences doesn't develop until a child is 18 years old or older.

What can you do? Your teen doesn't want to go on vacation with you, doesn't want even to be seen with you, and, quite frankly, you'd be happy not to include him in your weekend plans. And it's not like you can hire a babysitter for a kid who's old enough to drive.

The key bit is to be honest with yourself. Recognize when your kid is involved in activities you don't think are right instead of sweeping them under the rug. Know whom he hangs out with and what he and his friends do together. Dare to be the grown-up. Ask questions. Be a pest.

At the same time, remember that the whole point of raising a teen is to prep him for living on his own. His brain development requires opportunities to make important decisions. And you can't accomplish either of these important objectives by limiting his activities to the point that only the "right" choices are available.

No one ever said being a parent is easy and the trick of supervising teenagers while giving them the freedom they need and so dearly desire is one of the biggest problems a parent can have.

Consistent values, respect for your child, and healthy skepticism when your child tries to scam you are key. Get past this patch and things smooth out. You will want to have a good relationship to come back to. Keep your eye on that.

Brothers And Sisters
Should you have another?

Why First-Borns Get All The Goodies

It's true that over half the American presidents and a majority of Nobel prize winners were first-born children. This might make you think that there's something special about the juju that makes up that first embryo and that the raw material of follow-up siblings is just not so good. As a second-born child myself, I beg to differ.

What is different for first-borns is the situation into which they're born. Just a comparison of first-born and later-born baby scrapbooks will tell you: first-borns are the center of attention and later-borns not so much. First-borns have only adults to talk to. First-borns are fussed over and worried about. Everything first-borns do involves some major decision. It's hard not to think you're special with all that special attention. From first word to first day at school to first day of college, first-borns are the center of their parents' world.

Later-borns benefit from the experience their parents gained while practicing on Kid #1. They often live in a more relaxed world and have their older sibling to break the ground for them and show them how to manage the tasks of childhood and adolescence. So it's no wonder that later-borns tend to be not quite so driven, not quite so anxious for success, as their older brother or sister is.

Each spot in the family has its positives and negatives. The family is different for each child who comes along. It's not the same and doesn't seem the same to everyone in it.

Do Kids Naturally Go Separate Ways?

If the first kid in a family is "the smart one" does the second kid almost purposely decide to be "the funny one" even though she might be as smart as the first-born? Do kids unconsciously choose their roles in the family according to what's already been taken and what's left?

Think of your own family when you were a kid or the families of your childhood friends. If you had to assign a role to each person, what would it be?

Name   Birth Order   Family Role

Does there always have to be a "black sheep" of the family? What do you think?

Every Child A First-Born

The first child in the family enjoys the undivided attention of his parents. No matter what other distractions his parents might have, this kid gets all the attention his parents can spare. The key in raising Child #2 and #3 is to pay a similar amount of attention.

Later-born siblings have smaller vocabularies, on average, than first-borns. Since the number of words a person knows is related to his ability to grasp concepts, vocabulary is a key item. One thing you can do to support the development of your second and third children is to talk with them. It's easy to let the older child speak for all the kids—he is, after all, older and more articulate than his younger brother and sister. And in the hectic environment of most households, and especially households with several children, it's hard to find time for the explanations and discussions you had with Child #1. But talking with all your children, and listening to what each one has to say, is one of the ways you can give all your kids the advantages the first kid had.

A second suggestion is to remember that all children in the family are unique and not duplicates of each other. Sometimes parents promote a "family brand," like "We're the Jacksons and we all sing and play music." Take time to find out the interests of your younger children, just as you did for your first-born child, and don't assume that he's a clone of his older sibling.

Having siblings adds to the richness of family life, especially if everyone can shine. With every new child in the family, life gets more complex and it's hard to fit everything, and everyone, in. But treating every child like a first born is a good goal to have. We all want to be number one.

10 Tips For Babies In Bunches

For some families, spacing children is a moot point. If your children came in twos or threes or more, here are a few tips.

1. Get a schedule and stay organized.

2. Use time-saving devices even if you're a do-it-yourself kind of person. There will be plenty of time later to bake your own bread or whatever.

3. Cut back on outside commitments. Learn to say "no."

4. Accept help every time it's offered. Never say, "Oh, that's okay; I'll manage."

5. Treat your children as individuals, not as parts of a set.

6. Keep separate baby books for each of your children.

7. Don't make comparisons between them. Just like other siblings, kids who are twins or triplets develop on their own timetables.

8. Not everything should be shared. Kids need their own possessions, their own friends, and their own interests.

9. Expect that kids who are multiples may be slower to develop than singletons, since multiples are usually smaller at birth. That's okay. They'll catch up.

10. Find a twins group to hang out with. Only other parents of multiples really appreciate the fun and the challenge.

Close Together Or Far Apart?

Having answered the question, "When are you two going to have kids?" by producing a beautiful baby, you likely were immediately asked, "When are you going to have another one?" Good question.

To a certain extent, any attempt to plan the spacing between children is more wishful thinking than anything else. Planning children is a little like planning a picnic in Minnesota. Maybe it will work out.

But when children are spaced closer than two years apart, there is a greater chance that babies will be smaller than they would otherwise have been. More years between children are preferable to fewer years, up to a point. Getting pregnant at all in your late thirties is more difficult than getting pregnant at age twenty. And some diseases and conditions are more likely to affect older women and their babies than in earlier pregnancies. So biology is key.

Also, if you're a woman committed to a career, or if your family needs your income, then you might want to be away from the workforce as little as you can. You might decide to have only one or two children closely spaced. On the other hand, parents might not want to have two or three children in diapers at the same time, or that many teenagers in the house at once.

From the child's point of view, it's best to be established in kid society before having your place as the baby in the family taken over by somebody else. To children who are four or five, a new baby seems less like a rival for parental attention and more like just a curiosity.

Think about biological and economic factors, as well as what is best for the people in the family already. Then see what happens.

Competitors Or Collaborators?

Cain and Abel are one of the world's most famous sibling pairs and since Cain killed Abel, we can assume all was not rosy between them. But are siblings usually competitors? Here are some famous sibling pairs that at least were in the same line of work and often worked together.

Orville and Wilbur Wright
Ann Landers and "Dear Abby" Abigail Van Buren
George and Ira Gershwin (Composer/ Songwriter)
Groucho and Harpo Marx
John F. Kennedy and Robert Kennedy
Actors John and Joan Cusack
Brian, Carl and Dennis Wilson (The Beach Boys)
Tennis players Venus and Serena Williams
Football quarterbacks Peyton and Eli Manning
Comedians Tom and Dick Smothers
Singers Donny and Marie Osmond

The list goes on and on. Are you and your siblings in the same line of work? Do you think like your siblings, and do you like the same things? Write down your thoughts.

Sibling Rivalry

If a child has a sibling, she also has sibling rivalry. It's natural and normal. Even though you might be saying, "Oh, no, not my children," believe me, there is rivalry your kids just don't let you see.

Most people who have a sibling remember feeling that a brother or sister received preferential treatment from their parents. Many siblings still feel this way. Sibling rivalry is a reasonable outcome of two factors: scarce resources and a not-very-well-developed moral sense.

By definition, family resources are scarce. There is a finite number of cookies in the cookie jar. Sometimes those resources are doled out by chance, sometimes by need and sometimes they are doled out as a deliberate reward.

And by nature, children don't have a very well-developed moral sense. They tend to see things in black-and-white terms. Either you love me or you don't. Either I'm your favorite child or my brother is. If I can get more attention, then my sister has less. Children are self-centered.

How close children are in age doesn't seem to make much difference to sibling rivalry. And while some parents show blatant favoritism of one child, most cases of sibling rivalry aren't caused this way. There's just not a clear and consistent cause of sibling rivalry or a fool-proof way to avoid it. So the best course is to embrace sibling rivalry as a natural phenomenon and work around it.

Sibling rivalry usually fades as kids grow up and find their own niche in life. This is not to say that there aren't any destructive relationships between adult siblings—there certainly can be. But such relationships in adults are the exception, not the rule.

Sibling rivalry *in children* is normal.

Avoid Being The Wicked Step-Parent

1. Accept that this won't be easy for anyone and will take time. Don't rush to create "the perfect family."

2. Listen. Hear what's being said for the information it conveys and not as criticism. When a child says, "I hate this," she's saying she's unhappy. She needs support, not an angry response.

3. Be consistent without being rigid. Base decisions on a consistent framework or value system so that it's not difficult for kids to anticipate what you might agree to. Be on the same page with your spouse.

4. Recognize that children have a special bond with their birth parents, including the non-custodial parent, and make room for this.

5. Avoid playing favorites or making comparisons between the children or even appearing to do so. Be fair.

6. Model the behavior you want to see. Be cheerful, compassionate, patient, and accepting.

Step Sibs

Can children who began their lives in different families come together in a new, blended family without much difficulty? Of course. Does it happen very often? No.

Take a look at all that is going on when adults who have children from previous relationships combine households. First, each set of children must share their birth parent with a step-parent. This feels like a loss for them. Second, this new relationship absolutely squashes any fantasies about birth mom and birth dad getting back together and it may also change the children's interaction with their non-custodial birth parent. Third, each set of children must learn about the new parent and adjust to him or her and accept the authority of this new adult in their lives. Fourth, at least one set of children and often both sets of children move to a new home, so that their familiar setting is gone. Fifth, the children who moved to a new home must figure out new schools and make new friends. All of this upset happens and we haven't even talked about adjusting to new siblings yet.

So add to all that the new siblings. This can be a delightful experience, like a perpetual sleepover, or it can trigger near-murderous levels of sibling rivalry. Children are naturally on the lookout for favoritism, unshared privileges, and seemingly intentional slights. They naturally seek to dominate their birth parent's attention. A child may try to sabotage the relationship between her own parent and a step-sibling or even with the step-parent. Things can get really ugly really fast.

Even in biological families, there are personality clashes, difficult moments, and unhappiness. So don't be too quick to attribute rough patches to being a blended family. And avoid blaming the past. Avoid blaming a non-custodial birth parent. Deal with the present and move forward.

Make Your Child Feel Special

Every child needs to feel special. This goes double for siblings of children with special needs. What can you do?

- Make sure to have one-on-one time with each of your children, even if you have to put it on the calendar every week so you're sure not to forget.

- Appreciate the talents and charm of each of your children and tell them so.

- Little things matter: cook a favorite meal, play catch in the yard, go to a ball game.

- Show up at your child's school events, sports matches and performances. When you can't attend, ask your child to give you a point-by-point account of what you missed.

- Enlist the help of grandparents or even hired help to free up family time.

- Leave your child notes, text messages or phone calls.

- Listen when your children share their frustrations and longing for a more "normal" life. Help them deal with their feelings without making them feel guilty.

The Special Needs Sibling

It's one thing to feel competitive with your brothers and sisters. There's the feeling that they have it coming and the teasing, fighting, and subterfuge of sibling life is part of the fun of being a family. But when your sibling can't fight back, the dynamic changes.

Siblings of children with special needs can feel a little lost. Often their parents are stressed and worried. Often, time is devoted to medical care or therapy for the special needs sibling. Time, money and attention all seem to go the special needs sibling's way. The typically-developing child naturally feels left out and resentful and then feels guilty for feeling that way. Kids who have to cope with a special needs situation are just as egocentric as other kids. But they have to try to act as selfless and other-directed as a sensitive adult.

So it comes as no surprise that siblings of children with special needs crave extra support. They may need help in understanding their sibling's condition and prognosis. They may need help in finding ways to express their frustration and neediness without feeling guilty or being punished. And they need attention from their parents that is freely given and truly focused on themselves alone, not attention that is carved out of bits of time.

None of this is easy. If you're the parent of a special needs child, you already know how hard things can be. To realize that your other children also have a special need for recognition and attention seems to add to the stress you feel. It's easy to think that your other children should be able to see that there is only so much of you to go around and cut you a break.

But they are kids, so they can't do that. They are counting on you to make them feel special too.

Small Families Are Good For The Planet

Alan Weismann, in his fascinating 2007 book, *The World Without Us*, suggests that if all women had only one child, that would go far to save the planet.

He says that this idea, implemented right now, would reduce the human population by one billion within 50 years (instead of increasing it by 1.5 billion as would otherwise happen).

Within 75 years, the human population would be reduced by half, with obvious reductions in energy needs, toxic emissions and so on.

So having only one child might be not just a reasonable choice but a good idea.

Is One Enough?

Why worry about siblings at all? Why not just have a single child and be done with it?

Popular opinion has long held that only-children are different from other kids in unpleasant ways. People think only-children are spoiled, demanding, and socially inept. Even the noted psychologist Alfred Adler believed such things.

None of this has been supported by research. Research indicates that only-children are not all that different from children with siblings, except that they, like first-born kids with siblings, tend to talk more than other children and have a bigger vocabulary. Like all children, only-children benefit from lots of adult conversation. The difference for them is there is no other kid in the family interrupting them.

It's true that adults who were only-children may miss having a brother or sister to kid around with and to reminisce about "the good old days." But they also missed out on sibling rivalry and divided parental attention all that time they were growing up. If only-children appear to have had more advantages than children from larger families, it's probably because their parents had only one outlet for their time and money. Certainly parents shouldn't feel guilty about "depriving" their only-child of a sibling.

In short, there is no one ideal family size, no ideal spacing of children within a family, and no necessary connection between birth order and personality. Families are wonderful for the most part and are certainly essential, but the "ideal family" doesn't exist, never did and never will. Instead of chasing some notion of the perfect life, base your choice of family size on reasons that make sense to you.

Birds, Bees And Babies

What your child needs to know when

Inquiring Minds Want To Know

By about the time a child is three she will start to ask quite reasonable questions that parents may feel funny about answering, questions about babies but also about dead birds, beggars on the sidewalk, and the words for their own genitals. Questions about the realities of life seem to come long before parents think kids are ready to hear the answers. But inquiring minds do want to know.

Often we are embarrassed and don't want to answer. So we hiss, "Shh! Not now!" and hope the child will be distracted.

Or we answer but with a fantasy. We give our child's genitals cute labels, not the real ones. We say that the homeless person is bad. We say that babies come from their mommy's tummies and we don't know how they got in there. Our children are smarter than that. They know we're not being frank with them.

So we wind up creating intrigue around the very topics we want our kids to be less inquisitive about. We will get more questions, not fewer, and the questions will come when we least expect them and when they are most embarrassing. It would be better to answer truthfully the first time.

A good way to do that is by asking a question of your own: "What do you think?" You can then confirm or correct your child's idea. Doing this keeps your answer within the limits of his understanding and keeps you from answering with more information than your child wants.

How Did You Find Out?

When did you learn about how babies are made and how did that conversation come about? What do you remember about sex education programs at school?

Write about your experiences here.

Where *Do* Babies Come From?

So back to those three-year-olds, the ones whose mothers or whose friends' mothers are expecting a baby. What do you tell them?

Delightfully, you tell them the truth, the whole truth and nothing but the truth. Maybe not in one marathon conversation but as questions come up you tell the truth. Little kids—those who haven't yet started school and been exposed to the sniggering culture that exists around sex there—are scientists, not voyeurs. Children are fascinated by the facts, which are, when you think of it, pretty amazing. They will take what you tell them truthfully as information. They will be less embarrassed than you might be.

Naturally, you will break this information down and deliver it in bits over time. If your five-year-old asked you what makes a car go, you wouldn't tell him everything about internal combustion engines all in one go (even if you *knew* about internal combustion engines). You would tell him some today and let him think on that and come back later with another question. That's what you'll do in explaining about sex, too.

When you talk to your children about sexual matters, you should use the correct terms. The only reason to use baby-words for genitals is because you yourself have a hard time saying "penis," "testicles," "breasts," "vulva," and "vagina." Get over it.

And when your kids are older and have been taught by their friends that they should feel embarrassed by sexual information, the need for this matter-of-fact, all-questions-answered-truthfully plan is even greater. Be a reliable source that never asks embarrassing questions back. Accept that kids need to know and give them answers.

Family Legends

When my boys were quite young, I took them to Isle Royale in the middle of Lake Superior between Minnesota and Michigan for several days of backpacking and camping. To say this was a memorable trip is an understatement. The flamer-thrower camp stove, the terrible dehydrated food, and the weight of our packs have all become matters of legend. Family legend. Your family will have its legends too.

You can memorialize key events in your family's history by not only doing memorable things but by telling stories about them. How Mommy and Daddy met, how children were born or were adopted, the choosing of a pet, and the move to a new city all are the beginnings of legends that will bind your family closer.

My father's mother, who died long before I was born, once won a set of dishes in a hammering contest. I know this because of a family legend and I know a little bit about this extraordinary woman because of this snippet of the past.

A big part of being a family is contained in shared experiences and memories. Start right now to create with your kids family tales that will be told into the future.

What If My Child Is Adopted?

Of course adopted children need to know the facts of life just the same as kids raised by their biological parents. But adoptive parents can't very well say, "Mommy and Daddy (meaning themselves) so loved each other that they decided to have a baby and that was you." While the facts of reproduction remain the same, the storyline is different for the adopted child.

The wonderful fact of being chosen by adoptive parents is offset by the problem of having been rejected by biological parents. Even though rejection is not explicitly described in the story of how a child came to her adoptive family, the implication is that somehow the child wasn't wanted by her mysterious biological family. Fear of abandonment is universal among children. If I were abandoned once, what's to say I won't be abandoned again?

So in talking about adoption with your child, you need to exercise care and sensitivity. And deep down inside you too might fear being abandoned. "What if my child prefers her biological parents over me?" you might think. So there can be some defensiveness and anxiety that gets in the way on both sides. Professional guidance can help.

Another help is open adoption. If your child has enjoyed the company of her biological parents since birth, then your job is easier in explaining how the adoption occurred. There are real people involved, not fantasies, and there is no mystery about who these people are. If your child can just call up her birth mom on the phone or have her come over for a visit, things are much clearer for everyone.

The bottom line is that every person wants to be wanted. Make sure your child knows she is wanted and dearly loved. Include her story in the tales your family tells.

Become More Aware

Keep track of sexual references in messages aimed at children and teens. Notice clothing trends, commercials, television programs, and toys.

Write what you see here and give some thought to how you feel about this.

Walking The Talk

You know what's funny about American society? We are shy about talking with our kids about sex but we sexy them up from infancy on. We exploit our children's sexuality with toddler-size T-shirts that proclaim "Chick Magnet" or "Pimp" but would be embarrassed to explain to them what their own shirts say.

Carol Schiller, creator of the Baby Chaleco line of children's clothing, in which each piece features a whimsical animal or floral appliqué, reports receiving requests from some baby boutique owners to develop styles that are "edgier." Do you really want your child to be "edgy"?

We are concerned about child sexual exploitation from online predators, incest, and folks in the neighborhood but we also dress our kids provocatively and watch "family" television programs laced with snide jokes. You don't have to be a prude to wonder what's going on here. Why do we expose our children to so many casual references to sex?

Since our mantra in these pages has been "model what you want to see," try to model responsible and mature attitudes toward sex. You want your child to grow up to have satisfying relationships and that includes a sexual relationship with someone he loves dearly. You don't really want him to be promiscuous, to exhibit himself shamelessly, or cheat on his spouse and family. You want him to treat himself and others well.

While you cannot make these things happen in your child's future, you can at least ground his sexual development in your own behavior. Actions speak louder than words and your kids are watching your every move.

An Interview With Amy Lang

Talking about sexual matters with your kids shouldn't be a "hit and run," says sex education expert Amy Lang of Birds+ Bees+Kids in Seattle. It's not something you can do once, check it off the list of parental responsibilities, and forget. Not at all.

"Sex education is a health and safety issue," Lang says. You wouldn't tell your kids just once to be careful crossing the street or to eat their vegetables. Every day you reinforce messages that help your children be strong and happy. Sexual information must be included in those messages.

Lang also points out that you wouldn't wait for your child to ask about how to cross the street or why it's important to eat broccoli. You're proactive about those messages and you must be proactive in talking about sex too. You're the adult. It's your responsibility to make sure your child knows what he needs to know.

Kids going off to kindergarten should already know "all the body stuff," says Lang. Both boys and girls should know about menstruation and the mechanics of conception, fetal development and birth. They should also know that sex is "not for kids."

Lang also says that before children start middle school they should know about "everything, including pornography, oral and anal sex and STDs." The well-informed child has the knowledge to keep herself safe. The well-informed child knows what your expectations are for her sexual behavior.

It's never too late, Lang says. But the sooner you include sexual information in your casual conversations with your child, the healthier and safer she'll be.

Prepping For Puberty

Puberty comes a whole lot sooner than you remember it. Part of this disconnect is the fuzziness of memory. But part of it is that puberty *does* come earlier than it used to. A hundred and fifty years ago, girls didn't start menstruating until they were about 17. Today, breast budding occurs as early as age nine and a girl's period can start as early as age 10.

The reason is mostly due to body weight. A hundred years ago, nutrition was far more haphazard than it is today, and it took kids longer to reach the weight required for menstruation to occur. Today's children are not only better fed but in many cases they're over-fed. In fact, girls who have a high body-mass index at age three or who gain weight rapidly between age three and six can be predicted to experience early puberty.

Early puberty is also associated with being overweight in boys, although most of the research has concentrated on girls.

So though you thought you had until your kid was in fourth or fifth grade to have The Talk, you really need to discuss puberty much earlier. Expert Amy Lang suggests making explanations of menstruation, conception and pregnancy part of your occasional discussions of sex with your child from preschool on.

You want your children to learn about puberty from reliable sources, not from whatever their friends tell them. Many adults find this information difficult to share, especially with younger kids. Remember that your child will not share your queasiness but will view the information as merely interesting, at least if you offer it when the child is young. So talk about reproduction in small doses early and often.

Modeling Acceptance

You have preferences. You have opinions. And sometimes it's hard to recognize that other people have different preferences and different opinions and that those are *equally valid*.

But even if you find it hard to accept different preferences and opinions, you must accept *your child* whatever her preferences and opinions. At the point where discussion and even arguing leave off is where acceptance begins.

The issue might be sexual orientation. It might be politics. It might be religion. It might be what hue is an acceptable color for hair. Be ready to accept your child, no matter what.

Truly loving another means letting go of all expectations. It means full acceptance, even celebration of another's personhood.
        —Karen Casey, *Each Day A New Beginning*

What If My Child Is Gay?

Sexual orientation is something your child is born with. It makes as much sense to ask, "What if my child has blue eyes?" as it does to ask, "What if my child is gay?" Sexual orientation should matter as much to parents as eye color.

And it could if the world were fair. But as long as there's discrimination against gays and lesbians, there will be concern among parents. The concern, though, is not about how you can turn your kid straight. You can't. The concern is about how you can support your kid in an unfair world.

The first way to support your child is not to second-guess her sexuality from childhood on. Constant analysis of her preferences and interests for clues to her orientation will only make both of you unhappy.

The second way to support your child is to encourage her interests even if they are not traditional for her sex. You will do this for your straight children so do it for your gay child as well. Whichever of your kids wants to grow up to be a firefighter, a horse trainer, an artist, an actor, or a computer programmer is worthy of your support.

The third way to support your child is not to try to assign blame for her sexual orientation. Although sexual orientation, like eye color, is genetically determined that doesn't mean that one side of the family or the other is "at fault" for your child's homosexuality *or* for her green eyes.

The fourth way to support your child is not to tolerate intolerance in your relatives, in her school, or in any one else, including yourself. You child deserves the "unconditional positive regard" of the universe, to use the famous phrase of psychologist Carl Rogers, just as your other kids do. You are a big part of your kid's universe. Create for her the best possible world.

Just Say No?

Recall your own adolescent interest in sex and even your experimentation with sex as a teen or college student. What precautions did you take or not take against pregnancy and sexually transmitted diseases? Did you engage in sexual behaviors then that you wouldn't think of doing today?

Or were you a sexual "late-bloomer"? Did you feel out of step with your more active peers or did you feel your lack of sexual participation was a conscious choice?

Think back and see how your early experiences influence your thinking today about your own kids.

Sexual Decision-Making

Remember a few pages back when we noticed that the part of your kid's brain that gives him the ability to think ahead about the consequences of his actions doesn't develop until he's 18 or older? Remember that?

Put that together with adolescent *itchiness* and you'll see how easy it is for kids to make regrettable decisions about their sexual behavior. You can't chaperone your kid day and night. So how can you guide his choices at those times when his body is urging action?

Lay out consequences ahead of time. Find time to help your son or daughter understand that:

- STDs are forever and forever interfere with a person's love life.
- Oral sex doesn't eliminate entirely the risk of STDs.
- Pregnancy creates a monetary responsibility that lasts for at least 18 years.
- A baby affects a person's immediate future plans as well as plans for the next two decades.
- A baby creates a link to the child's other parent that can't be undone.
- Even a choice to abort the pregnancy or put the baby up for adoption does not undo the psychological effects of creating a child.
- Drugs and alcohol cloud judgment.
- Teens who have sex with someone younger than the legal age of consent (17 in many states) can be arrested.

Please remember that it's not effective to launch into a long lecture at any time and especially not as your kid is heading out the door for a big date. Find teachable moments throughout your kid's preteen and teen years to talk about sexual decisions. Start early and repeat often.

Age-Appropriate Behavior

Girls mature faster than boys. Popular culture contributes to girls' early interest in sexual attractiveness, dating, and marriage. A quick look at age-old stories, like *Cinderella* and *Sleeping Beauty*, confirms this, as does a trip down the "pink" aisle in any toy store. So don't be surprised if your kindergarten daughter comes home with a crush on some boy in her class.

But it's a long way from kindergarten to the mid-twenties, the age at which most young women marry these days. Don't rush things.

Parents feel a tension between wanting a fairy-tale princess sort of popularity for their daughters and wanting girls to "save themselves" for marriage. You can't have it both ways. And given the range of opportunities for young people these days, opportunities based on a good education and a sense of independence, it's a smart idea not to hurry to pair your kid up.

What You Want For Your Child

Goodness knows, it's hard to see the forest for the trees sometimes and that's never truer than when thinking of your child as a sexual being. Most of us just want to put a lid on the entire discussion or get so hung up on bits and pieces that we forget to remember the whole point of parenting, which is:

To raise competent, well-adjusted children who move smoothly and effectively into their adult lives.

Part of adult life is having a satisfying and reciprocal sex life. A kid doesn't get there by figuring everything out for himself. Not when his parent could point him in the right direction.

But there's a difference between "pointing him in the right direction" and "directing his love life." You won't like every date your child brings home. You will like some dates more than he does. Your kid will make some choices you think are deplorable and miss some opportunities you'd grab in a heartbeat. But this is his life, not yours. You are there to guide him out of harm's way, if you can, but you're not there to prevent him from ever making a mistake.

Your child will have his own reasons for choosing the person he chooses. The factors he considers important might not be the ones you think are important. But you don't want one of his main criteria in choosing a mate to be "the person who will annoy Mom and Dad the most." You don't want to make his romantic choices a demonstration of who has the most power because when it comes to choosing whom to love, the power is all on your child's side.

Concentrate on your own love life and let your child develop his.

Discipline
Developing your child's self-control

What You Want To Happen

Imagine your child as a teen-ager. She is tempted to do something wrong. Obviously, you want her to make the right choice, but you also want her to make the right choice *for the right reason.* You don't really want her to choose the right way just because if she doesn't, you'll ground her for a week. You want her to choose the right way because she knows right from wrong and she selects the right action *because she wants to.* You won't always be around, ready to direct and correct her behavior. You want her to grow up to be a responsible, thoughtful adult you can be proud of.

This sort of self-discipline is your real objective in training up your child.

So disciplining your child is less about what's happening right this minute and more about developing long-term ways of thinking and acting. Even though you only have what's happening right this minute to go on, your eye should always be about developing a responsible person for the future.

Discipline is less about obedience and more about self-regulation. Developing self-regulation and self-discipline takes a while. There will be mistakes made. But your patience and your consistent effort will be rewarded.

Values Chooser

Which values are important enough to you that you want to develop them in your child?

Orderliness
Top priority   moderately important   not important at all

Kindness
Top priority   moderately important   not important at all

Goal-direction
Top priority   moderately important   not important at all

Competitiveness
Top priority   moderately important   not important at all

Spirituality
Top priority   moderately important   not important at all

Dedication to work or a cause
Top priority   moderately important   not important at all

Community
Top priority   moderately important   not important at all

Independence
Top priority   moderately important   not important at all

Ecology
Top priority   moderately important   not important at all

Social justice
Top priority   moderately important   not important at all

Respect for authority
Top priority   moderately important   not important at all

What else? _____

Your Role

Just because what you're aiming for in your child is self-discipline, that doesn't mean that you can just let your child figure out right and wrong all by himself. You've got a big role to play.

You establish what's important in your family. You do this intentionally or you do it without thinking. Either way it happens, but obviously being intentional is a good idea. So your first order of business is to know your own values. What's important in your family?

Aim for big ideas, instead of small ones. You might want your child to pick up after himself, not to fuss about brushing his teeth and to put his clean clothes away. But if you have a family rule for each of those, you'll wind up having to have a new rule for every itty bitty situation. A better course is to have a few broad principles: "In this house, we are orderly. We keep our spaces neat, we do things on time, we keep ourselves and our things clean." If orderliness is important to you, make it a valued quality and the day-to-day applications of this quality will fall into place. Your child will be able to apply this quality to other situations going forward in his life without having to have a parent create a rule for it.

So think of the four or five Big Things you want your child to use as guiding principles. Orderliness might be one or you might not care so much about that. What do you care about?

You and your child's other parent are the leaders in your family. Decide on the general direction you want to go.

Helping Kids Get Along

A recent study found that fewer than 10% of three- and four-year-old children shared candy with another child, but that 45% of seven- and eight-year-olds did. What surprises you here? Is it that preschoolers don't share very much? Or is it that second-graders don't?

Most parents think their children can share, but probably those children really don't share much in their daily interactions (at least not when candy is involved). We can't take for granted that kids know how to behave.

How consistently does your child:

Share?

Help others without being asked?

Take turns?

An interesting study suggests that pro-social behavior actually *decreases* as children get older. So maybe you should ask yourself how often *you* share, help others, and wait your turn patiently.

Remember to model what you want to see.

How Kids Think

Your values hit reality when you try to get your kid on board. Why is it she doesn't seem to understand what you want her to do?

Young children don't think like adults. Their brains are not developed enough for them to think the kinds of thoughts adults do—in fact, not until 18 or 20 do kids' brains develop to the point that they can pretty confidently predict the consequences of their actions and plan ahead to avoid disaster. Eighteen or 20!

Small children (kids under five or six) can't really understand another person's point of view. They tend to believe that everyone thinks the same thoughts that they do. This is why young children cannot lie or keep a secret very well. They don't realize that the person they're talking to doesn't already know the truth. They can't understand that everyone has different thoughts.

Young children are stuck in the present moment. They have difficulty waiting their turn or understanding what a promise is because they don't "get" the future. They can't think ahead. And they also can't look back. It's hard for young children to learn from their mistakes because they don't have long term memories until well after age three. If you ask a three- or four-year-old to remember what happened "the last time you tried that stunt," he will give you a blank look. He doesn't remember.

And children of all ages are pretty self-centered. They can be jealous of a sibling or mean to a friend, not because they are bad children but because they don't think beyond themselves. Part of your role is waiting for maturation to catch up with the social niceties but a bigger part is patiently teaching basic ways of getting along. Kids aren't being dense or intentionally difficult. They're just being kids.

Discipline Tracker

What method of discipline do you use most often? Keep track for a few days.

How often?

Slapping _____

Spanking _____

Yelling _____

Speaking angrily _____

Shaming _____

Giving a time-out _____

Grounding _____

Threatening _____

Taking away privileges _____

Taking away food _____

Locking out of the house _____

Assigning chores _____

Ignoring the child _____

Ignoring the behavior _____

Tattling to someone else _____

Letting consequences occur _____

Explaining _____

Negotiating _____

What changes might make you more effective?

Why Punishment Doesn't Work

The fact that young children don't think the same way as you and I goes a long way toward understanding why punishment doesn't work very well. Kids are bad, not because they mean to be bad, but because they can't see beyond their noses.

What children need is instruction in how to behave, but punishment is a blunt instrument. Punishment tells what not to do, but it doesn't tell what's okay to do in a similar situation. So punishment tends to be effective only in the present moment. It stops the behavior now but it doesn't prevent it in the future.

Punishment can lead to a perverse sort of 20 Questions. The child calls his mother a "doo-doo head" and gets yelled at. Next time he's angry, the child—who knows that "doo-doo head" is forbidden—calls her a "poopy-brain." And on and on. Eventually either the parent gives up and wonders how she gave birth to such a rude kid or the child clams up and decides that mom really doesn't care that she keeps making him so angry.

A better course is to go back to your values. If a value in your family is "Treat people kindly," then mom can respond to being called a doo-doo head by saying, "It's not nice to call people names." She could even go on to supply an okay way of expressing anger. "You can say, 'That makes me so angry!' instead of calling me a name."

Other favorite punishments, like the Time-Out Chair, also fail to teach the behavior you do want and don't do a good job of inhibiting the behavior you don't want. Punishment like that involves you in a game of control (*can you make me stay on this chair?*) when your authority as the parent should not be in doubt. Your authority lies in your values. Reinforce those.

The Proper Way To Praise

Praise works best when it is about the job or outcome, not the child. So

"I really like how you used the color blue"

is much better than

"You are a good artist."

Notice how you praise your child. Most of us tend to praise the child instead of the outcome. It takes practice to learn to tell what you like about the accomplishment instead.

Write down what you notice here.

Why Promises Don't Work

It is not true that people do things only because they will be rewarded for doing them. What is true is that every person has an inborn desire for respect. No one—not even a child—wants to be manipulated. When rewards and promises are used to coerce good behavior, children revolt. No reward is better than being an independent, free person.

This doesn't mean you can never say, "Wow, that was a terrific thing you did. Let's celebrate!" But it does mean that you can't develop the kind of self-discipline you're looking for when you say, "If you do a terrific thing, then we'll celebrate." The problem is not with the celebration but with the cause-and-effect condition put on it. A celebration is something you do *with* another person. A reward is something you do *to* another person. No one wants to be done-to.

Kids can be bought, yes. You can get a child to clean up her room by promising to take her to the movies. But you won't develop her sense of responsibility, only her sense of power. The next time you want her to clean up her room, she will ask, "What will you give me if I do?" Now it is she who is doling out rewards and you whose behavior is being manipulated. Was this what you had in mind?

If not, then go back to your values, not straight to the rewards and promises. Try saying, "Gee, this room is a mess! In our family, we try to keep things neat. I wonder how quickly you can get this straightened up?" If the mess is huge, make the task child-size by limiting it to picking up the clothes or just the Barbie stuff. If you can, reinforce the value by cleaning up the kitchen while your child works on her room.

And when you see what you want to see, celebrate.

Offering Choices

Practice giving choices instead of orders. See how this works out for you. In addition, be sure to model what you want to see happen.

Day 1
Instead of ordering my child to...

I gave a choice between ...   and

The result was ....

Day 2
Instead of ordering my child to...

I gave a choice between ...   and

The result was ....

Day 3
Instead of ordering my child to...

I gave a choice between ...   and

The result was ....

Control Issues

It's frustrating being a parent. It seems like kids should do as you say. Blind obedience would make family life so much easier. But blind obedience doesn't develop responsible adults who can live successfully on their own. And you do want your kids someday to move out and live on their own, don't you?

A well-disciplined household with polite and responsible children is not achieved by giving orders and demanding compliance. In order to develop your children's *self*-control you have to give up some control yourself. You have to give them enough room to make wise choices and to learn from their mistakes when they make less-wise choices.

Shared control happens at each child's developmental level, of course. No one is suggesting you let your four-year-old set his own bedtime and find out tomorrow that he feels like sleeping through preschool. But you can say, "It's nearly bedtime. Wrap up what you're doing in the next five minutes, please." You're making the decision on bedtime, but your child isn't summarily told to go to bed; he's given a few minutes to finish what he's doing.

When you can give choices, do so. Asking, "Do you want to wear your blue shirt or the yellow one?" gives a two-year-old enough autonomy (sometimes) to allow you to get her dressed. Asking your ten-year-old if he'd like to do his math homework or his spelling first gets past his resistance for doing it at all.

Sometimes parents think they shouldn't have to be so subtle with their kids. Isn't just telling them quicker and better? No, it's not.

Do As I Do ... Sometimes

What are the things you do that you'd most like your kids to copy? What are the habits you have that you'd really like your kids to ignore?

My Good Side	My Bad Side

Children have never been very good at listening to their elders, but they have never failed to imitate them.
—Novelist James Baldwin

Being A Role Model

The apple doesn't fall far from the tree.

Not only is your child *genetically preset* to behave a whole lot like you—which is scary enough, when you think about it—but your child from the very beginning learns how to behave *by watching what you do.*

Whether you like it or not, you are a role model. Basketball star cum sports commentator Charles Barkley is famously quoted as saying, "I'm not a role model," forgetting that it's not up to him. It's the people who know a person who make that decision.

And children do look up to their parents. Preschool and school-age children adopt their parents' views and try to be like them. They notice things about their parents that even their parents don't notice in themselves.

Like lying, for instance. Po Bronson, writing in *New York Magazine*, notes that 98% of teenagers say they lie to their parents routinely. Even though honesty is the number one quality nearly every parent wants for his children, nearly every kid lies. Why? Bronson says it's because they see their parents do it. Kids learn to lie by copying their parents.

No one is saying you have to be perfect. It's hard enough just being reasonably decent. But you are being watched and you will be emulated. So if you gossip, yell at your spouse, cheat on your taxes, lie on your resume, hit the dog and say mean things about the neighbors, don't be surprised when your kids do the same.

You can say all you like that you're not a role model but it's just not true. The truth is you are.

The Liminal Zone

I travel quite a bit, speaking to parents and such, and for me airports are a liminal zone—a sort of no-man's-land where the rules are suspended. All those nasty fast foods, trashy magazines, and duty-free shops are a temptation to throw nutrition and budgets to the wind.

Do you have a liminal zone when it comes to your kids? A time or place where you do things you'd never agree to do in your "real life"? For some parents, their liminal zone is when they're on vacation. For others it's holiday gift-buying time. For others it's whenever their child is sad or unhappy. At these times and places, many parents spend with abandon and do things or make promises they wouldn't make any other time.

Liminal zones are the enemy of consistency. It takes real self-control to keep them from taking over and making every day a fairy-godmother day. Where are your liminal zones?

I tend to over-indulge my kids when...

Consistency Pays Off

Rules may be made to be broken but when it comes to raising self-confident kids, consistency pays off. A five-year-old I know, a child as interested in cool stuff as any other boy, can walk into a toy store, look at all the merchandise and walk out again when his mother says it's time to go with never once asking her to buy something or making a fuss. Far from being deprived, this child seems to enjoy these excursions thoroughly. His mother's secret? From the get-go she has never bought a toy in the toy aisle. It's just not something that is ever done.

This may seem like consistency in the extreme but it illustrates the point. Children look for any chink in your armor, not because they are in a battle for supremacy but because they are supremely self-absorbed. If they can get their way, they will. And the moment you say, "Okay, just this once," is the moment you open the door to hearing, "You let me before."

Let's get real here. No one can be consistent all the time. And especially as your child grows older, you will want to negotiate privileges with her so she can have more room for making choices and seeing consequences. But if your answer to a simple request ("May I have a cookie before dinner?") is sometimes yes and sometimes no, you will get the request every day just to see what the answer is today, and you will get louder protests when you say "No." If the answer to cookies before dinner is always negative, kids give up asking.

Consistency applies also to those values you've set as the guiding principles for your family. If courtesy is important to you, you've got to drive your car in a courteous way. You can't expect your kids to do as you say but not do as you do. Actions speak louder than words.

Spanking's Wrong? Says Who?

If we really want a peaceful and compassionate world, we need to build communities of trust where all children are respected, where home and school are safe places to be and where discipline is taught by example.
—Desmond M. Tutu, Archbishop Emeritus

Children should never receive less protection than adults. . . [we must] put an end to adult justification of violence against children, whether accepted as 'tradition' or disguised as 'discipline'.
—Paulo Sergio Pinheiro, Member of the UN Sub-commission on the promotion and protection of human rights

I have never accepted the principle of 'spare the rod and spoil the child.'... I am persuaded that violent fathers produce violent sons... Children don't need beating. They need love and encouragement.
—Gordon B. Hinckley, President,
The Church of Jesus Christ of Latter-day Saints

Corporal punishment of children actually interferes with the process of learning and with their optimal development as socially responsible adults.
—Daniel F. Whiteside, Assistant Surgeon General,
Administration of President Ronald Reagan

Punitive measures whether administered by police, teachers, spouses or parents have well-known standard effects: (1) escape—education has its own name for that: truancy, (2) counterattack—vandalism on schools and attacks on teachers, (3) apathy—a sullen do-nothing withdrawal. The more violent the punishment, the more serious the by-products.
—B. F. Skinner, Ph.D., Professor of Psychology, Harvard

Corporal punishment trains children to accept and tolerate aggression. It always figures prominently in the roots of adolescent and adult aggressiveness.
—Philip Greven, Professor of History, Rutgers University

Never, Ever Hit A Child

No matter who tells you it's okay—and there are some well-regarded nutcases out there who will tell you just that—it is never okay to hit a child.

Stop and think. What does getting into a barroom brawl tell the world? That you've lost all control of yourself and have let your baser passions take over. You deserve a trip to the county jail and to have your name printed in the morning papers.

And what does it tell the world when you hit a three-year-old or an eight-year-old or even a fourteen-year-old? That you've lost all control of yourself and have let your baser passions take over. Don't fool yourself into thinking that hitting a child is the only way to get through to him or that he was asking for it or that God wants you to hit children. Hitting children is evil, plain and simple.

That's not to say that parents don't do it. Studies show that a majority of parents think spanking is okay or at least admit to hitting their kids. These same parents are baffled when their kids hit and kick their classmates, when they are mean to their siblings and when they grow up and hit their parents back. What do they expect?

If you raise a child in violence you are contributing to the violence in our society. You are part of the problem, not part of the solution. If you hit your child, don't blame video games or R-rated movies or the neighbor's kids for making your child unruly. You did it yourself.

Me, Myself And I
Your child forms an identity

Getting From Point A To Point B

Even babies have personalities and opinions. They each pop out of the womb with a unique way of reacting to the world, and soon they shape their parents' actions to suit their preferences. So it's not that personality is created as much as it's *revealed*.

But at what point does the child herself realize that she is a separate individual who can act independently of her parents? At about 18 months, toddlers can recognize themselves in a mirror. They can touch a spot of ink on their faces that they know is there only by seeing their reflections. Two-year-olds notoriously exercise their independence by saying "no" even to things they want.

But once the thrill of throwing tantrums wears off, a child tends to be a follower more than an insurrectionist. School, sports and friendships all require the child to go along with what is asked. The elementary-age child pretty much adheres to rules and accepts authority. So how do kids get from the point, at about age eleven, of being dependent on adults to the point, ten years later, of being ready to move out on their own, get a job, get married, and become an authority figure themselves?

It's clear to see that the transition might not be smooth. We authority figures may not be happy to be dethroned by teenagers. But we *want* our kids to become self-sufficient. The question is how to make this happen without losing any sleep.

The Identity Timeline

18 months	Recognizes himself in a mirror
2-3 years	Wants to do everything himself
3-5 years	Aligns with his gender role and knows "what's appropriate" for boys and girls
7-8 years	Understands that others don't know what he knows unless he tells them
8-9 years	Starts to compare his performance and abilities to those of other kids
9 years	Starts to develop a "trait orientation" which means the child believes there are qualities he has and things he's good at and qualities he'll never have and things he'll never be good at
10-11 years	Begins to realize that his parents make mistakes and are not completely in control of things
10-12 years	Peers start to become more influential than parents
11-12 years	Begins to wonder how he will ever manage all the tasks required of an adult
12-15 years	Sexual identity is shaped and sexual attractiveness becomes more important
15-17 years	Peer opinions increase in importance
15-17 years	Own ideas become more important and every idea comes under scrutiny, particularly his parents' ideas
16-18 years	Sexual or romantic experimentation helps to define who the child is
17-21 years	The child develops a temporary or working belief system

How It Goes

It starts with sulking and whining. "Why can't I do that? Everyone else can. You're so mean!" Doors slam. Things get thrown. Tears and swear words. Sneaking behind your back. This is your child when she still believes she has to do as you say but doesn't like what you just said.

This nasty stage doesn't last all that long because your child soon comes to believe that she can ignore your opinion altogether. She doesn't ask for permission anymore and you have to mount a full-scale interrogation to find out who are her friends and where's she's going. Twelve-year-old tantrums are replaced by fourteen-year-old cold stares, shrugs and silence. Your opinion counts for nothing. You just don't understand.

Later things sweeten considerably. Your seventeen-year-old will smile tolerantly and tell you what you want to hear. She no longer needs to make a scene or even show her contempt. She knows that she is, at long last, in charge. She lies with perfect credibility—not wanting to cause you any pain and worry—and then does whatever she was going to do anyway.

The ages of these stages may be slightly different for your child. Her highs and lows may be flatter or steeper than these. But just about every adolescent progresses down this path as she moves from your control to her own. This will be a test of your ability to model the behavior you want to see.

Try your very best to meet that challenge. Stay pleasant as much as you can. You don't want to reinforce tantrums with yelling or meet her cold shoulder with exasperation. Expect that your older child is not being frank with you all of the time. (Notice that neither are you with her.) Celebrate the progress that is being made toward adulthood. It *is* a good thing.

When Did You Rebel?

So, which sort of rebel were you as a teen? Were you:

A Rebel Without a Cause
The Eternal Child
The Compliant Child
or
The Mature Kid?

Remember your relationship with your parents and also the relationship your brothers and sisters had. (You might have been Compliant, but what about them?)

Write your thoughts here about the development of your own sense of identity.

Why Rebellion Is A Good Sign

Why do teens need to rebel at all? Why don't they just agree that we parents know far more than they do?

Rejecting parents' values is an essential step in growth toward being a real adult. According to psychologist Erik Erikson, everyone must reject his parents' values and develop his own. Erikson concedes that a person might wind up *recreating* his parents' values but the process of rejection and creation is essential. Only that way can a person become a mature individual.

So that means that when your teen seems to reject everything you stand for, it's actually a positive step in the process.

There are four outcomes of this rejection/creation process. We can give these some labels to make them easier to remember:

The Rebel Without a Cause: This is the kid who has successfully rejected his parents' values but hasn't yet developed his own. Right now he's steering without a compass, and we all hope he grows up soon.

The Eternal Child: This is the kid who hasn't rejected his parents' values *or* created his own. He is stuck with the personality development of a nine-year-old and might need a push.

The Compliant Child: This kid has not rejected her parents' values but she has created her own. Since she hasn't rejected her parents' values, though, her values are just a clone of Mom's and Dad's. She knows what she believes in but hasn't a clue why.

The Mature Kid: This person has rejected her parents' values *and* successfully created her own. She knows what she believes in and she knows *why*. She is ready for adult responsibilities. Bravo!

Finding Time To Talk

How can you find a time when you and your teen can listen to each other? Here are some ideas.

Eat dinner together. Every night is ideal, but if not every night then plan a parent-child standing dinner night every week. Go out to eat at a low-cost but nice place where it's not too noisy or too crowded with her friends. Or eat at home. In that case, cook together.

Cook dinner together. If you can chop vegetables without getting violent with your kid, then choose an interesting recipe and cook it together.

Talk in the car. The great thing about the car is you don't have to look at each other, the driver is busy and can't strangle the passenger, and the conversation is over when you get to your destination. I don't recommend that you try to talk while *your child* is doing the driving.

Go for a walk. Go round the block if you like, but even better is walking at the park or somewhere there might be interesting things to see. Walking while shopping certainly is an option.

Play games together. Shoot some hoops, play video games, play tennis, whatever. During the play or in the pleasant time after the game is over, there's time to talk.

Forced Choice

Your role as the parent of a teen is quite different from your role as the parent of a younger child. You must actually help your child cut the apron strings and learn to think for himself.

Cutting the apron strings is as hard for parents as it is for some kids. You fully realize the dangers of being on one's own and you also have a really good imagination and can think of dangers that aren't even likely. It's even easy as a parent to *thank your lucky stars* if your teenager still goes along with whatever you say and seems pretty much the same as he was when he was a little kid.

But it's not good for him. Your job as a parent is to bump your child out of his comfort zone and get his feet under him. You really do want him to stand up and start making decisions, even bad decisions. Remember that the last big piece of brain development happens in the teen years and it's dependent on thinking hard to make choices.

For many teens, the rebellion part is easy. It's the creation of a personal value system that's hard. Many teens are easily led into extreme ideas, cults, goofy notions and exploitative situations as they seek truths they can believe in. Teens can be passionate about these ideas. So your task as a parent is to influence your child's thinking without forcing him into a corner. You don't want a fight to the death over loony ideas. Doing that will only make him defend them more strongly.

So the teen years are a key time for interesting, not angry, discussions over dinner. Shared family dinnertime has been shown to be a key factor in developing mature behavior in teenagers. Even if family dinners are out of the question, find time to have lively discussions with your teen about current events, books, and popular culture. Help him develop his ideas in a supportive atmosphere.

The Sorcerer's Broom

Do you remember the story of "The Sorcerer's Apprentice"? Mickey Mouse played the apprentice in *Fantasia*. In the story, a wizard's serving boy succeeds in making a broom come to life, but then he can't control it. He tries to chop it to bits but the bits just become more brooms and make more mischief. The poor apprentice can't get ahead of the train of events that he set in motion.

Trying to get ahead of the danger-of-the-day is like that. By the time parents figure out what mischief teens are in to and take steps to warn them away, the kids are on to something new. Adults can never quite catch up.

So building a sense of responsibility and that elusive ability to foresee the outcome of one's actions is the only certain way to safeguard kids against dangers you can't even imagine. Long before your child will be tempted (which means long before she gets to middle school) give her chances to make small decisions. Let her see how things come out and evaluate her choices.

Doing this with small decisions over time during childhood will give your child the skills she needs to think things through later when risky temptations come her way.

Risky Business

If you have ever smoked, dabbled in drugs, or drank beer or harder stuff you probably remember the first time you did any of those things and the reason you tried them. Most likely the reasons included wanting to go along with a peer who already used them and also simple curiosity.

Kids who "turn to drugs," as the phrase goes, don't do it to be delinquent or even to experience the high or buzz. The first time is more social or experimental. And once kids are past the first time, the second time is easy. That's why using is such a risky business.

You can see that your child's reasons for trying risky behaviors are the same impulses you've encouraged throughout his childhood: appreciation of good friends and a lively interest in the world. So what can you do now that these prosocial impulses are tinged with danger?

First, avoid adding to the reasons:
- If you use, don't indulge in front of the kids.
- If you use, don't share things with your children, not even the Thanksgiving sherry.
- And don't be so harsh and restrictive that doing drugs, drinking, and smoking are made attractive as ways to get back at you.

And then, do what you can:
- Talk to your kids about substance abuse, early and often.
- Pay attention and if you find evidence, ask nicely about it.
- Notice their friends who are using and ask about them too.
- Listen but expect to be lied to.

Kids outgrow this fixation on substances if they live to grow at all. It's worth it to keep trying until that happens.

Who Are Your Child's Friends?

See if you can fill in the blanks. If you can't, it's time to find out the answers, in a nice way of course.

Who is your child's "best friend"?

Which kids does your child spend the most time with?

Where do these kids live? Are they nearby or a distance away?

Is your child a member of some clique or group?

What do your child and his friends do for fun?

What is the riskiest thing your child and his friends do?

On a Saturday night, where are your child and his friends?

How often do your child and his friends attend school? Are his friends often absent or tardy?

Trading In Mom And Dad

Think about it: your kids will live in a world populated by their peers. It's their peers they must connect with. So eventually they will move beyond the family sphere and make their own families and their own lives.

In the meantime, though, there can be trouble. In the gap between childish connections with family and adult connections with peers, kids can fall into peer connections that are childish and not adult at all. They can trade in the guidance of Mom and Dad for the influence of bad companions. How can you guide your kid through the dangerous gap between his childhood family and his adult future?

Of course, guidance starts long before your kid hits his teens. Knowing right from wrong is built over a long time. Ideally, you want this pretty much internalized by age 12. If your teen still has an angel and a devil arguing on his shoulders when he's old enough to drive, you, he and the rest of society are in trouble.

But that's water under the bridge. If your kid is a teenager already, then be sure to invite his friends in and let them hang out some, so you can size them up. This doesn't mean, though, that you become just another pal. Keep the lines of communication open, but also be ready to draw the line on what can be done in your home and what can't.

Help your own kid by helping the kids he brings by. Be a role model and a reliable adult. Teens are well aware of how dangerous the neighborhood can be. Provide safety by providing structure and a vision of what being an adult looks like.

There will be lapses. But outgrowing you is the last step in your child's development. Make it happen.

Sleeping
Getting past the struggle

How Much Sleep Is Enough?

The answer to this question is easy enough.

- Newborns need 15 to 18 hours per 24-hour day but get this in a series of two- and three-hour naps, not in a "night's sleep." (Oh, you noticed!)
- Infants between four and nine months old sleep 14 to 15 hours per day, including naps.
- Children ages one to three years old need 12 to 14 hours, including naps.
- Children three to six years old need 11 or 12 hours total. Threes might nap but sixers don't.
- Children seven to 12 years old need 10 to 11 hours.
- Teens 13 to 18 need 9 hours or more each night, which they are likely to get between the hours of midnight and 9 am, if they have the chance.

But many children miss these targets. From toddlerhood on, most kids sleep *a full hour less* than what is required. So does that matter?

Yes.

Lack of sleep is related to poor school performance, crabby behavior, aggressiveness, ADHD, and even obesity. Because things learned during the day are encoded in the brain during sleep, the sleep-deprived child is not as smart as he would be with more sleep. Now you know why you want your kids to sleep more—you thought it was so you'd have more peace and quiet, but it's even more important than that.

Sleep Tips

Back before central heating was common, experts on child rearing suggested bedroom temperatures of 50°. Brrr! No wonder people wore night caps.

Here are more modern tips for children's sleep comfort.

Set the bedroom temperature at about 64° F.

Use cribs manufactured after 1970, when safety standards were improved. Don't use an antique crib.

Check the bolts and connectors on all beds to make sure they stay tight. Don't allow jumping on the bed since that can weaken bed supports.

Be careful with bunk beds. Make sure the bed is sturdy and that chances for falling are minimal. Bunk beds shouldn't be used for kids younger than four.

Be wary of very soft mattresses and pillows. Opt for firmer surfaces and bedding that doesn't envelope a sleeper. Sleeping with one's head under the covers isn't a good idea. If your child's head gets cold, turn up the heat a couple degrees.

Look for quality and support in choosing mattresses, even for children.

Let most of the stuffed animals sleep on a shelf. Make sure there's room for your child to stretch out and move around in bed.

Where To Sleep?

When your kids are not getting all the sleep they need, ask yourself, "Where they are when they're not getting it?" Maybe they're in their own beds, but maybe they're somewhere else.

There's a small percentage of families that are committed to co-sleeping, with everyone in one big bed. But there are many more families that have separate beds for everyone that not everyone uses. In some households, children start the night in their own beds, then wander into their parents' bed sometime in the wee hours, not just occasionally but every night. In other households it's a parent who sleeps in the child's bed on pretty much a nightly basis. In other families, kids with separate bedrooms end up all in one bedroom, either sleeping on an empty bunk or curled up at the foot of a sibling's bed. And let's not even consider the kids who spend the night in the dog's bed or who fall asleep on the couch each evening and spend the night there.

The long and the short of it is that even though people may say everyone sleeps in his own bed, in actual fact this doesn't happen all that often. That's fine if it works, but if children aren't sleeping well or if adults are kept awake night after night, then it might be time to reconsider the sleeping arrangements.

If it's time for a change, then you'll get some resistance from your children and you'll get it in the middle of the night when you're least likely to be at your best. So talk through the new plan and the reasons for it during the day when everyone's more agreeable. Remind the kids of the new plan before bedtime. And during the night, stick to your guns. It will take a few nights of consistent reinforcement to make the new sleeping locations work, but work they will. Don't you feel more rested already?

Bedtime Dos And Don'ts

You want your child to fall asleep easily. So in the hour before bed...

Do feel free to include:
    A bath or shower
    A glass of milk
    A story
    Quiet play
    Low-key television programs
    An evening walk
    Sitting and talking with a parent
    Reading in bed for a limited time

But try to avoid:
    Video game play
    Work that takes a lot of brain power
    Active play
    Scary stories or television programs
    Arguments and upsets
    Cola drinks and other caffeinated foods
    Large meals
    Watching television in bed

There never was a child so lovely, but his mother was glad to get him asleep.

—Poet Ralph Waldo Emerson

The Go-To-Bed Routine

Sometimes the problem isn't getting your children to stay in bed but getting your kids to bed in the first place.

If your child is an infant under six months old, your baby will not sleep as long at one go as you'd like. Even though people ask you, "Is he sleeping through the night yet?" don't think that there's something wrong that he's not.

As for letting your infant cry, remember two things: picking him up will not reinforce crying behavior and babies cry because they're unhappy, not to manipulate you. So pick up your child and try to get him settled down. Remember that being tense and angry will only add to his upset, so find a way to stay calm.

Toddlers and older kids benefit from an evening routine that is predictable and not too stimulating. Avoid video games and competitive play after dinner, opting instead for gentler entertainments. Playing board games is fine as long as it's friendly and not too mentally or emotionally taxing. If your older kid has homework, see if she can get it done before dinner so the evening hours are not burdened with that stress.

Once in bed, kids should stay in bed. Establish a one-time-up rule and stick to it. Second times out of bed can be met with stony silence and an escort back to the bedroom. Reading in bed is fine, but watching television is not, and make sure lights are out within 20 minutes or so of bedtime. Studies show that even a night-light can disrupt sleep so at least turn off the main light in the room.

If your three- or four-year-old struggles to fall asleep it may be that she should give up her nap. This is a sad day for the parent who likes that break in the afternoon, but cutting out the nap can make the night times easier.

Famous Early Risers

If you're up early with your child, you can try to make the best of it. Here's some advice from the past.

Early to bed, and early to rise, makes a man healthy, wealthy, and wise.
> —Statesman Benjamin Franklin

I never use an alarm clock. I can hardly wait until five a.m. In the army I always woke before reveille. I hate sleeping. It wastes time.
> — Science fiction writer Isaac Asimov

Sleep is an acquired habit. Cells don't sleep. Fish swim in the water all night. Even a horse doesn't sleep. A man doesn't need any sleep.
> — Inventor Thomas Edison

Easy for them to say, you're thinking. So catch a nap, if you can.

I usually take a two-hour nap from one to four.
> —Baseball player Yogi Berra

Up With The Bluebirds

Right up there with getting kids to bed and getting them to stay there through the night is getting them to stay asleep past dawn. If your toddler or preschooler has a tendency to awaken all bright-eyed and ready to go at 4:30 or 5:00 in the morning, know that you're not alone in having your day start way too early. Like the birds outside the window, little kids seem programmed to wake before the sun is fully up.

Unless you're an early riser too, you may want to do what you can to tweak your child's schedule. Make certain that he is not going to bed too early and push bedtime later if necessary. You might try room-darkening shades in the nursery. Older kids who can't stay asleep even though their bedtime seems appropriate might need to cut out a nap or be more physically active during the day.

Having a routine time for getting up is helpful here, just like having a routine bedtime. As soon as your child is old enough to read a digital clock, you might try teaching him when it's okay to emerge from his bedroom. Quiet play in his room is permissible as long as you can be certain that he can't get into trouble.

Having a routine time for getting up helps to set your child's internal clock, which is what you want to happen. But this means that your child will not sleep in on the weekends. Being the parent of a small child does mean that you're up and doing on Saturday and Sunday, same as on Monday.

Children do grow into a more-adult pattern of sleep. By age five or six your child will be sleeping longer in the morning. In fact, in adolescence, kids' internal clocks reset so that they naturally sleep far into the morning and are awake far into the night, which makes waking with the bluebirds seem preferable after all.

143

Dream Content By Age

Children ages three to about five dream of simple things, like a bird. These dreams don't seem to have any story behind them.

Children ages seven or so include themselves in their dreams and also include other people they know. Their dreams tend to be located in familiar situations.

Children ages eleven to thirteen start to dream in complex story lines that might be allegorical or symbolic. Now children can dream memorably fantastic dreams that seem "to mean something."

Do you remember a dream from your teen years that has stuck with you all this time? Describe it or draw a picture of your dream image here.

Sweet Dreams And Nightmares

We can guess that babies dream. Newborns experience much more REM (rapid-eye movement) sleep than do adults and REM sleep is associated with dreaming in adults and children. So babies probably dream. We just have no idea what they dream about.

By about age three or four, children can describe having a dream, though they are not entirely sure what was going on. Young kids have difficulty telling fact from fiction. For them, the dream is "in the room." As far as they're concerned dreams are not in their heads but right there, actually happening in their bedrooms. No wonder small children are unnerved by their dreams of big dogs and monsters.

Older children, who understand that they can think thoughts, are more easily convinced that dreams are not physically real. But even for them bad dreams can be upsetting and cause for sleeping with the lights on.

Kids' dreams don't need interpretation, and if you think you can figure out what triggered a particular dream for your child, you should probably keep this knowledge to yourself. But notice if dreams seem to recur or make your child anxious. Nightmares and disturbing dreams can mean your child is under some sort of stress during the day. See if there are things going on that you can smooth out for your child or that might be helped by a heart-to-heart talk.

There is also evidence that bad dreams can be caused by scary plots and disturbing images in movies and video games. If your child is troubled by dreams, dial back his media consumption and monitor more closely the content of what he does watch. Scary entertainment isn't fun if it keeps everyone up at night.

REM Sleep Explained

Not all of our sleeping hours are the same. Brain activity varies in repeated cycles during the night. Adults experience a complete sleep cycle about every 90 minutes, so that eight hours of sleep contain about five cycles.

The sleep cycle is divided into REM sleep and non-REM sleep. REM sleep is the period when dreams occur. Brain activity during REM sleep is about the same as it is when you're awake. But during REM sleep you're unable to move around.

The proportion of REM sleep is related to the total hours spent sleeping.
- A baby, who sleeps about 16 hours out of 24, spends 50% of her sleep time in REM sleep. That's eight hours a day.
- A preschooler, who sleeps about 12 hours in a 24-hour day, experiences 25% of that sleep as REM sleep.
- Adults who sleep eight hours a night devote about 20% of that to REM sleep.
- Elderly people, who might sleep only four or five hours a night, get only 15% of that as REM sleep.

If a person is deprived of REM sleep—by being constantly awaked by a newborn, for instance—she will dream more and dream more vividly when she finally does get some REM sleep.

REM sleep seems necessary for forming memories and solidifying what was learned during the day. So get your REM sleep and see that your child sleeps well too.

Night Terrors And Sleepwalking

"Daniel, Daniel! What's the matter?" Daniel sits bolt upright in bed, eyes open in the dark, screaming and yelling at the top of his lungs. Mom shakes him gently but he continues to holler. He flaps his arms and trembles, seemingly terrified, and he won't stop, and he won't say what's wrong. After at least 10 minutes of this (what must the neighbors be thinking?) he subsides and allows himself to be tucked back in. Trembling herself now, his mother goes back to bed. The same thing has happened every night this week.

This is a night terror. It's not the same as a bad dream. Night terrors occur in the deepest levels of sleep and it's nearly impossible to awaken a child or get him to stop. Children who experience night terrors often are in some anxious situation during the day. One way to make them stop is to figure out what is upsetting the child and fix that situation.

Another way is to intercept the night terror before it starts. Because these episodes usually happen early in the night at about the same time each evening, you can sometimes head them off by waking the child up just before a "scheduled" episode. Breaking the cycle often works.

Another nighttime difficulty is sleepwalking. This is not usually a problem because if you find your child out of bed you can lead her back to bed. But some kids sleep walk right into trouble, so be sure the doors to the outside are closed or locked at night.

The tendency to sleepwalk seems to be hereditary. Like night terrors, it's most common in early childhood. Kids usually grow out of both sleepwalking and night terrors. But until they do, you will need to be prepared to guide your not-really-conscious child back to bed.

A Break In The Action

If not a nap, then downtime of some sort is good for everyone. Instead of rushing straight from school to piano lessons on Monday, straight to karate on Tuesday, and so on, try to plan in half an hour or so for your child just to catch his breath.

One of the criteria for creativity is time to think.

If you and your child have been living too hectic a life lately, try scheduling in time for nothing. You might find that this takes some getting used to. But see what new ideas and solutions occur to you when you just hang out and let your mind relax.

Write down what happens here:

Naps

Considering how much parents like a nap when they can get one, it's funny how eager children are to give them up. Toddlers who clearly are running on empty resist falling asleep and defiantly declare that they are not tired at all.

Kids used to nap more than they do now. In the 1950's and 60's, kindergartens (which met for only half a day) always included naptime. Today, even Head Start programs for three-year-olds have deleted the nap. Part of this can be attributed to the hectic pace of modern life, with something going on every minute. The boredom that used to send young kids to bed each afternoon just doesn't exist anymore. And part of the lack of napping can be attributed to lack of insistence on napping. Where once kids were sent to their beds for an hour each day at 3:00, whether they were tired or not, now parents hesitate to impose such an arbitrary requirement. The long and the short of it is that if we lament the loss of naptime it is something we've brought on ourselves.

There's nothing wrong with imposing a nap requirement and there's a lot to be said for some downtime during the day. If you want to make a nap part of your child's daily routine or if you think he needs it, then simply plan for it. Clear your schedule each day so a nap can happen; at the designated hour, pull down the shades, turn off the TV and the telephone, and let everyone rest. Older kids (and you) might not sleep but might spend this time reading, though there's nothing that says they can't sleep.

Children who nap regularly will need to wean themselves away from this delightful habit in time to attend full-time school. And at that point, the child's bedtime may need to be adjusted to add in the sleep that used to be got during naptime. By the same token, children who have trouble getting to sleep at night may not need their naps and should be kept active in the afternoon.

Help Your Sleepy Teen To...

1. Recognize her limits. She may have to prioritize her activities and not do everything she's doing now.

2. Be as efficient as she can with homework and other tasks. Provide a good workspace, computer access, or other support so she can get her homework done without wasting time finding materials.

3. Dial down activities in the evening so she can be relaxed by 10 pm even if she's not asleep then.

4. Understand her sleep needs. Most kids are not aware that nine hours of sleep is the ideal for them.

5. Sleep in on the weekends. Some of her sleep debt can be made up with extra sleep when she can get it.

6. Cut out caffeinated drinks and other chemical interferences with sleeping well.

7. Rearrange her schedule if she can so that she doesn't need to be anywhere—or be at her best— early in the morning.

Up All Night, Sleep All Day

Younger children sleep at night and are up during the day, pretty much like Mom and Dad. Teens run on hamster-time, whirling around on the teen equivalent of an exercise wheel in the wee hours of the morning. Teens prefer to sleep till noon. Why is that?

Children's circadian rhythms change during puberty, caused by a difference in when during the day the hormone melatonin is released. The evolutionary value of this change is an interesting question. Why did Mother Nature decide it would be good for teens to be up when their elders are asleep? No one seems to know. Whatever the reason, we're stuck with it. Teens stay up late and prefer to get up late too.

This can raise obvious problems in the evening, as Mom or Dad lies awake, watching the clock and listening for Junior to come home from wherever he is. By definition, there's less supervision of teens when the older generation is in bed.

But the shift in teens' sleep cycle is a problem in the morning too. Teens still need more than nine hours of sleep each night. But the opening bell of most high schools rings between 7:20 and 8:00 am. Allowing for an hour to get up, get dressed and get to school, teens must rise by 6:30 or 7:00 am. Counting back nine hours yields a bedtime of 9:30 or 10:00 pm. Even on "a school night," it's asking a lot to expect a teen to be asleep by 10 pm. Given the importance of afterschool activities, a part-time job, and homework, it's hard to imagine fitting all that in before 10:00 pm anyway.

Teens need a break. They need to get the sleep their bodies require at the time their bodies will cooperate and feel sleepy. Fixing this problem takes some creativity.

What About Bed-Wetting?

Most children stay dry at night by the time they're four years old. Of the kids who continue to wet the bed, most will outgrow this problem eventually on their own. They need patience and some precautions and just time.

About 3% of middle school students have trouble with bedwetting, though. This problem affects boys more than girls. Most children who continue to struggle with this have a parent who also wet the bed.

If this is a problem for your kid, no matter what his age, punishment is not the answer. He's not doing it to be mean. Be supportive, help him change the sheets, and see what you can do that will have a positive effect.

- Limit beverages in the evening.
- Protect the mattress so bedwetting is less of a nuisance.
- Suggest he wear disposables if he wishes.
- Get medical advice. There are hormone treatments that can help.
- Help him train himself to wake up if he's a deep sleeper. Use an alarm clock or wake him up yourself for a bathroom break in the middle of the night.

Bedwetting is a nuisance but it's not the end of the world. It will either go away or your kid will find ways to deal with it. Your support will help him, either way.

Sleep Disturbances In Older Kids

Some older children and teens have trouble staying asleep at night or have trouble getting to sleep at all. Sleep deprivation can cause a host of problems, including sleepwalking, twitching eyelids, and disturbing dreams when the child finally does fall asleep. Poor sleep habits have even been linked to obesity.

Sleep problems in older kids can be caused by several things. Here are some possibilities to consider and solve.

Sleep apnea
This is waking caused by lack of oxygen, sometimes occurring several times a minute throughout the night. Snoring can be an indicator of sleep apnea. Sleep apnea happens when the airway is blocked by a person's tongue. It occurs most often when the person is very overweight or has swollen tonsils.

Chemical interference
People who smoke, drink caffeinated or alcoholic beverages or take some medications (like Ritalin) can have difficulty falling asleep. In addition, premenstrual changes in hormone levels and hormones released in stress also can cause insomnia.

Depression
Inability to sleep is a sign of depression but so is sleeping too much. If your child is struggling with sleep, an evaluation for depression is a good place to start.

All of these causes of insomnia can be helped. Since brain development picks up in adolescence, it makes sense to get help for your child if he has trouble sleeping.

Food For Thought
Thinking about eating

Clean Hands, Please

Everyone knows you should wash your hands before eating. We don't have to be told that a frightening number of illnesses can be caught by ingesting germs along with a jelly sandwich. Some of these illnesses can be severe, especially in small children, but in all cases illnesses contracted from germy fingers can cause runny noses, diarrhea or vomiting. Not what any parent wants.

Yet think of how often during the day your child goes directly from playing on the playground to nibbling fruit snacks. How frequently she sits in a shopping cart, clutching the handle that every other child has touched, while simultaneously munching popcorn. How often you and your child grab a bite at the local fast food outlet without cleaning up first.

The sketchier and more informal our eating habits, the more likely it is that kids will forego washing their hands before eating. Studies show that fewer than half of the families with elementary age children eat dinner together on a regular basis. That means that the routine of washing hands before dinner is also overlooked.

No one is suggesting that you become germ-phobic. There is intriguing evidence that exposure to nature in all its dirtiness *improves* the immune system and protects against allergies and asthma. But there's a difference between playing outdoors and eating with grubby hands after playing outdoors. Your child should play all he likes. Then wash up.

Are Foods For Kids Good For Them?

A recent study reviewed the nutritional content of 367 foods marketed as being especially "for children." None of these foods was candy, cookies or beverages. All of them were purchased at a regular supermarket.

Nonetheless, the study found

High salt	in 17%
High fat	in 23%
High sugar	in 70%
High proportion of calories from sugar	in 70%
"Poor overall nutrition"	in 90%

Despite the poor nutrition in these products, 62% of them advertised their "good nutrition" on the front of the package.

It would be easy for a parent to be fooled. Don't let it be you.

Nutrition Counts

Malnutrition isn't linked only with poverty. Plenty of U.S. children in otherwise thriving families are not thriving nutritionally. One reason is simply that entire families are not eating well. Another reason is that children fill up on nutritionally-poor foods and have no room left for the good stuff.

Preschoolers need complete protein, vitamins, iron, and calcium every day. Protein can come from dairy foods, meat or a combination of grains and pastas. Vitamins come from fruits and vegetables (fruits alone are fine if your child won't eat many vegetables). Calcium comes from milk and other dairy foods but also oranges and vegetables like broccoli. Iron is found mostly in red meat. Kids who don't eat meat might need an iron supplement in their multivitamins.

So this doesn't seem all that hard. How is it that kids can still be under nourished?

Feeding children is a zero-sum game. Anything a child eats that is not nutritionally sound takes the place of foods that are nutritionally sound. It's not that children eat too few good foods. It's that they eat too many bad things—and those take the place of good foods. Kids' stomachs are small. If they consume soda, cookies, candy, and French fries they will by necessity eat fewer foods containing protein, vitamins, iron and calcium. Imagine that everything your child eats every day has to contribute to her good health. Nothing should be included that isn't healthy.

This is not easy in today's culture. It means the whole family has to eat well. But nutrition counts for everyone.

12 Tips For Dealing With Picky Eaters

1. Serve foods everyone likes. This is a no-brainer.

2. Add controversial ingredients last, so your child's portion can be served without them. If your child hates an ingredient, don't serve it to her.

3. Don't worry about vegetables. Just be sure to serve fruit.

4. Don't permit complaints about food at the table. It's okay for your child to say, "No, thank you" but not to fuss and whine.

5. Encourage your child to try new foods. But don't make a federal case out of it.

6. Avoid pressure, bribes or punishment. Never turn meals into a power struggle.

7. Don't make dessert an issue. See #6 above.

8. Cut down on afternoon snacking.

9. Allow a bedtime snack if your child is hungry. But make it small and healthy, like a glass of milk.

10. Don't make your child clean his plate. When your child says she's finished, she is. But she should stay at the table, engaging in conversation until others are finished.

11. Keep meals pleasant. Talk about fun subjects unrelated to food.

12. Don't discuss what your child eats when she can hear you. Don't let her know she's got your attention with this.

You Can Lead A Child To Peas...

The average adult has 10,000 taste buds but your child has only one—the taste bud devoted to hot dogs (or maybe cookies or peanut butter).

Okay, that's not correct. Children actually have more taste buds than adults and their taste buds are more sensitive than adult taste buds, which have been dulled over the years. So children taste things more intensely. Rather than risk tasting something yucky, they figure it's safer to stick with just hot dogs.

Infants are born predisposed toward sweet foods (breast milk is sweet) and predisposed against bitter foods (many poisons are bitter). So it should come as no surprise that children prefer fruits to vegetables, not to mention candy, cookies and ice cream over vegetables. So you can lead a child to peas, but you can't really make her eat them.

Children are conservative eaters but their sense of culinary adventure can be cultivated. Chantal and Shane Valentine, owners of Alina's Cucina, a web-based cornucopia of tasty ideas for family dinners, researched recipes from around the world. With their pediatrician's blessing they developed ethnic dishes for their baby and found that family foods for children can be flavorful and interesting. Adventurous eating is undermined by serving the same things all the time. Mix things up a bit!

Kids' tastes do grow up. A young nephew of mine once explained his new appreciation of broccoli by saying "taste buds change." He was right, of course. So once in a while offer a formerly-rejected food again, maybe in a new way. Sooner or later (and sooner if you don't make a big deal of his eating habits) your child will expand his repertoire.

How Do You Use Food?

Notice how you use food with your kids. How often do you promise a treat for good behavior? How often do you use food as a reward? Do you make up celebrations in order to treat yourselves?

Keep track for one week:

What could you do instead of using food as a reward or comfort?

Not A Reward, Not A Comfort

Do you have a favorite "comfort food"? Most of us do. A comfort food is something that makes us feel safe and happy when we eat it—something we eat when we need a little comforting.

But this is different from using food as a distraction. Some of us do this too. When we're feeling blue we eat the whole carton of ice cream or drink the entire bottle of wine. Using food to disguise feelings doesn't make bad feelings go away. It only adds to our difficulties.

So resist the temptation to train your child to use food as a distraction. Instead of offering a Band-Aid and a lollipop when a knee gets scraped, offer a Band-Aid and a hug or a Band-Aid and a story. Being sad shouldn't be a reason to eat junk food.

And neither should good behavior be rewarded with food. How we reward people demonstrates what we think is important and valued. By using food as a reward, we distort food's importance. And notice the kinds of foods we tend to use as rewards: not carrot sticks but ice cream cones. So not only does using food as a reward distort the importance of food in general, it sends a message about what foods we value more than others. It's always the wrong ones.

If you are concerned about childhood obesity or if good nutrition is important to you, avoid using food as a comfort or as a reward. You don't want your child to believe that the "best" foods are the kinds of things that are used as rewards or that feeling down is an excuse to run amok in the snack aisle of the 7 Eleven.

Just because that's how you were raised doesn't make it a good strategy.

Check Your Shopping List

What beverages do you buy your kids? How much of each do they drink each day, at home or in restaurants?

Plain water

Flavored water

Reduced-fat or non-fat milk

Whole milk

Fruit juice

Fruit-flavored drinks

Soda

Smoothies

Milk shakes

Energy drinks

Sports drinks

What do you think of what you found out?

Washing It Down

Water is good for you and good for children.

Breast milk is the best food for babies. Babies who are breast fed past one year have the best advantage in health and cognitive development.

Older kids need the calcium, vitamin D and other nutrients in milk. Nothing substitutes for milk in a child's diet.

Fruit juices are tasty and provide some vitamins but they provide little good to offset their calories and sugars (even 100% juices are mostly sugar and water).

Juice blends and soda really have no place in a healthy diet. Not only do they contain sugar (or sugar-substitutes which are quite as bad for people as sugar itself), but they also reduce the amount of water and milk a child drinks. Sugary drinks deliver a nutritional double-whammy. Not only that but soda interferes with bone development.

This is all pretty straightforward. Kids should drink water and milk, period, with maybe a single glass of juice each day. So why isn't that what children really drink?

Children will choose sweet drinks if they have a chance— fruit juice, powdered drink mixes, soda, chocolate milk. Kids who drink sweet stuff regularly are heavier than kids who drink only milk and water. Not only that, but children who drink *diet* soda have a significantly higher body mass index than children who do not drink the stuff.

It's easy to overlook what children drink when thinking of how to feed them. But beverages can have a significant effect on kids' health. Be aware.

How Many Calories Is Normal?

A teenager can eat you out of house and home. Even younger children need proportionately more calories than adults to keep up with growth and keep an active body moving.

How many calories is typical?

Children 2 to 3 years need 1000 to 1400 calories.

Children 4 to 8 years need 1400 to 1600 calories, which is about the same as sedentary adult women.

Girls 9 to 13 need 1600 to 2000.

Boys 9 to 13 need 1800 to 2200, which is about the same as sedentary men.

Girls 14 to 18 need 2200, which is about right for active adult women.

Boys 14 to 18 need 2200 to 2800, which is about the same for active men.

Eating Disorders

When the world seems out of control, as it often seems to teens and young adults, managing food intake is one way of taking charge. Kids who develop eating disorders are often kids who are struggling with identity issues or who are under other stress.

Anorexia and bulimia are conditions with a strong psychological component. If your child is affected by these conditions, it makes sense to seek medical help. Just worrying about the food part of things is not effective.

What should you look for?

Children with anorexia have a distorted view of their bodies. They see themselves as much heavier than they are. What they see in the mirror is not what's really there. They may eat very little and excuse this as dieting or staying in the right weight for a sport. They may exercise to excess as a way to control weight. And they will deny that they have a problem. Since these children have a distorted image of themselves, they are telling the truth as they see it. The risk of starvation is quite real.

Children with bulimia are also obsessed with food intake but in the opposite direction. These children binge eat, devouring whole packages of ice cream or cookies at one sitting. They then force themselves to vomit and repeat the cycle. The binge-and-purge habit can damage internal organs and erode the esophagus, leading to serious medical problems.

If your child seems overly concerned about his weight and especially if he is also involved in an activity in which a desirable weight is important (like gymnastics or wrestling), be on the lookout for behavior that crosses the line from concern to obsession. Then get help.

Family Dinner Ideas

Cook something together, with everyone contributing.

Go to a farmer's market earlier in the day and pick out interesting vegetables to try.

Do a sort of Iron Chef challenge, based on the popular television show. Take turns each week, presenting a new food to cook and try out. Be sure the rest of the meal is tried-and-true favorites.

Make family dinner night Comfort Food Night and serve only food favorites.

Have a super dessert on Family Dinner Night.

Eat only appetizer-type foods.

Get take-out.

Try the most interesting microwave meals you can.

Make Family Dinner Night Soup Night. Homemade or canned or carry-out soups are delicious and easy.

Let your teen be the chef (You be his sous chef and help with the chopping and clean up).

Make Family Dinner Night Sandwich Night. Create great sub sandwiches or other favorites.

Have a taco bar with lots of different toppings.

Make Family Dinner Night Grill Night.

Take turns inviting someone in for dinner on Family Dinner Night.

Family Dinnertime

It's easy to pass off the importance of eating together as a family as ridiculously old-fashioned and hopelessly out of touch with modern life. Many households today do not even have a table large enough for all the family to sit around.

But studies consistently show that kids whose families eat together on a regular basis do better in school and stay out of trouble more than kids whose families typically eat on individual schedules. Something happens around the dinner table that doesn't happen anywhere else.

Experts advise making family dinner part of the regular schedule at least one night a week. Eating together provides an opportunity to appreciate each other's company, to shape table manners gently, to polish a child's ability to make pleasant conversation, and to reinforce other social niceties. Family dinner is an event hosted by parents for their children. It's your best opportunity to lead by example and suggestion. Why would you pass up this chance?

If you haven't had family dinner time in a long time you will feel some resistance. Your kids, your spouse, and even you will feel like this is too much bother. So start small. Commit to only one night a week (Sunday night is often chosen) but commit to that night every week for a couple months. It will take a while to establish the new habit.

Turn off the television during dinner. It's not really "family dinnertime" if you've invited a TV personality to hog the conversation.

Try it. I think you'll like it. And family dinners can make a difference in your children's success and in your role as a family leader.

167

Keep A Food Log

Keep track of what your child eats every day for a week (or keep track of yourself). There will be ups and downs, so an entire week gives a better picture than just one day.

_____

Monday

_____

Tuesday

_____

Wednesday

_____

Thursday

_____

Friday

_____

Saturday

_____

Sunday

All Things In Moderation

So. Can children never have a French fry or a piece of candy? Can kids never have a soda?

No. It's not that they can never have these things. And it's not that every meal needs to be perfectly balanced. But the diet of American children is so out of whack that thoughtful parents can't just feed their kids what every other kid eats. Because most children in this country eat junk.

Kids need breakfast and breakfast should include a non-sweet protein food. Although breakfast could include something sweet, not everything should be sweet.

Lunch should include a protein food too and also fruit or veggies that the child actually will eat. Starches—bread, pasta, or grains—should be whole grain. The same goes for dinner: protein, fruit or vegetables and whole grains.

The standard beverage should be milk or water.

Snacks should likewise concentrate on whole grains, fruits, or proteins. Opt for foods that are not manufactured whenever you can.

If all this is your child's standard diet, then there is room for the occasional (once a week?) serving of French fries or a piece of candy. On a special occasion a child could drink soda. But if your child's daily diet includes French fries, cookies, candy, soda, and other sugary, fatty foods, then there are real problems on the way.

Assuming your whole family eats healthily, your child will not feel deprived. She will learn to eat good foods and to permit herself treats once in a while. All things in moderation, yes, but most things should contribute to good health.

Children's Bad Habits
Annoying, disgusting and embarrassing

Whose Idea Was This?

Kids do things that their parents wish they wouldn't and they do them habitually. Children suck their thumbs, suck a pacifier, carry around a filthy blanket, pick their noses, bite their nails, masturbate, and pull out their own hair. Children have always done these things and undoubtedly always will.

Many of the annoying, disgusting and embarrassing habits children have are things that come naturally. Infants in the womb suck their thumbs. Masturbation is naturally pleasurable. When there's something bothersome in one's nose, the reasonable thing to do is pick it out. So kids can't really be blamed for having these habits.

Other habits which parents wish kids would give up are actually habits parents themselves introduced. No infant has ever gone to Walgreens and bought himself a pacifier. Mom and Dad did that and popped it into baby's mouth. Parents are often the ones who introduce the idea of a favorite blanket or stuffed toy. It's parents who tuck Fuzzy Wuzzy into the diaper bag or the stroller tray. It's parents who first insist on "the right" blanket for Junior at night.

So we shouldn't be surprised when children develop bad habits or when habits that we thought were okay when our child was little linger on until we think she's too old for them. Habits are natural. It's what to do about them when they start getting in the way that counts.

Did You Have A Security Object?

I'll confess. I had a blankie that I loved. I still remember looking at it wistfully on the top shelf of the closet. My mother stowed it there when she decided I was old enough to give it up.

How about you? Do you remember giving up a security object? Maybe you still have it in a drawer somewhere. Maybe you sucked your thumb long enough to recall doing that, or you chewed your fingernails. Maybe you still do.

Write what you know about this aspect of your past.

How Old Is Too Old?

Most parents have no trouble with an infant sucking on a pacifier. But when a preschooler has to pull his pacifier out of his mouth to explain the plot of a *Dora the Explorer* episode, most adults suspect things have carried on too long. At what age is a child too old for his favorite habit?

The child is too old, or is beginning to be too old, at the point when his habit becomes a habit instead of being a real comfort. A pacifier or a thumb for an infant provides real comfort. The suckling reflex is one of the few outlets an infant has for her anxiety or discontent. But at a certain point, the thumb or pacifier loses its comfort value and crosses the line into being a mere habit. The child sucks, not because sucking makes her feel good, but just because that's what she does. It's a habit.

It's true that an older child might suck his thumb particularly when he is falling asleep or after he's been upset. So it might appear that sucking still offers the same benefits it did when he was tiny. But actually the child has other outlets and could grow beyond the infantile suckle reflex. But because sucking has become a habit he will need some help to change.

Many adults retain their childhood habits but they've learned to indulge them in private. For them, a habit is more a matter of timing than age. In one study over 95% of adults admitted to picking their noses. They just don't do it right there in public.

Another indicator that a child is too old for her habit is if she says she wants to quit or if she is being teased about it. If a habit interferes with your child's happiness or reputation, then clearly she needs some help with it.

.

How Easy Was It For You?

Have you quit a habit? How easy was that?

If you've ever smoked cigarettes, used language that embarrassed you, left your clothes on the floor where you took them off, or said, "You know?" all the time, remember how you stopped doing those things. Or have you tried and not managed actually to quit?

Recall how hard it was to give up your habit and what worked for you. Write your thoughts here.

Goodbye To Binkie

How can you help your child give up a habit that needs to be let go?

If the habit truly must be stopped (not just moved to the privacy of one's own room), then it matters whose idea this is. If stopping the habit is the child's idea, then your job as a parent is easier. You and your child can brainstorm ideas for substituting something else for the habit, tracking progress toward reducing the habit and so on. You can be on a team, but the child takes the lead.

If stopping the habit is your idea, then you have two tasks: first you must make the child aware of when she is indulging in the habit since she's likely not aware of this, and second, you must help her to make the choice to reject the habit when she notices she's indulging in it. Noticing that she has a problem comes first.

Have a heart-to-heart talk someday when both of you are in a good mood and have some time. Describe your concern about the habit and state clearly your desire that your child give it up. Agree to notice how often she indulges in this habit over the next day or two. You might keep a chart or tally. Say, "Sally, I see you biting your nails right now" and have her mark the chart. But don't hassle your child when you see the habit happening.

At a second talk with your child, discuss the tallies on the chart and think of ways to reduce the habit. See if every day the number of indulgences can be smaller than before. Talk about other things your child could do when the urge to indulge the habit strikes. Work together on this, but not as adversaries. While quitting the habit might be your idea, you cannot make quitting happen without your child's cooperation. So cooperate.

Quitting takes time. Be patient and persistent.

Knock First

If there is a time and place for everything, then it's important to respect that by knocking on closed doors before entering.

Allowing kids privacy is troublesome for some parents. If you suspect that what's going on behind closed doors is illegal or dangerous then you want to open the door and walk in. But knock first.

Consider what household rules you want to establish about what goes on under your roof. What can you tolerate in privacy and what can you not? Write your thoughts here.

A Time And Place For Everything

Some childhood activities can be pursued in private or in a setting that appreciates them. As we've said, picking one's nose is something that even adults do, just in the privacy of their bathrooms (or cars). Playing with genitals is a normal activity for young children, and it's probably futile to try to stop it. A better course is to state that this activity must be done in one's own room.

Boys' delight in bathroom humor hits around kindergarten age and continues for several years (some would say for life), to the mortification and annoyance of adults in the vicinity. This presents an opportunity to teach that how we talk depends on whom we're with and the setting and situation. What's okay to chortle over with friends in the backyard is inappropriate at school or in front of Grandma. This is a valuable lesson.

Polite topics for the dinner table are different from topics discussed at a sleepover. Slang and profanity are best enjoyed with liked-minded friends, not with parents.

Remember that it's not possible to control your child's every move and utterance. What you can insist on is that she knows how to get along in the world. This means understanding that there is a time and a place for everything and she must wait until the time and place are right.

Teaching this fact is not teaching your child to be deceptive. There is no need for your child to hide what he is up to and it is not a good idea for him to think he must hide it. What you are teaching is that your child should respect the sensibilities of people around him. This is courtesy.

We all want courteous children.

See Things Clearly

The hardest thing to do is to see your children as they truly are instead of as you wish them to be. No one wants to think that a kids' home life or school stresses or hereditary predispositions have led to alcoholism, substance abuse, or self-destructive behavior. It's easier to ignore the signs or pass them off as just youthful experimentation. But denial helps no one. If your child has problems, they *will* surface, and when they do you'll wonder why you didn't pay attention earlier. The signs were there.

What to watch for:

- Disinterest in things that used to be important
- Furtive behavior and excuse-making
- Paraphernalia of all sorts
- Sleeping too much or too little
- Looking sick or actually feeling chronically unwell
- Missing valuables or prescription medications
- A drop in school attendance and performance
- Inability to keep a job, if the child is working
- Interest in cover-ups, like mouth wash, incense, and car fresheners

When A Habit Isn't A Habit

Some repeated activities are not so much habits as expressions of anxiety. Working with these is a whole different thing.

Hair pulling to the point of creating bald spots is in this category. Nail biting is too. So are head-banging, holding breath until the child is blue in the face, and cutting or scratching himself. All of these activities involve hurting oneself. That makes them indicators of anxiety and emotional distress.

For these activities, just being aware of the habit and working to stop it isn't enough. The source of the anxiety has to be addressed and resolved. In severe cases, where the child truly endangers or disfigures himself, professional help is essential.

In less-severe cases, figuring out what might have caused the anxiety and working with the child to alleviate that might help. Kids who chew their fingernails might start this after a move to a new neighborhood or after starting a new grade at school. Helping your child with this transition can help reduce his nail biting. Nail biting can become a habit, though, and continue after the event that caused it has been resolved.

Alcoholism can appear in the teen years, and when it occurs so young it's usually genetically triggered. If there's a history of alcoholism in your family, be on alert for this in your teen. And if your teen already drinks excessively, get medical help. This problem will not just go away.

In helping your child with a habit, be alert to the possibility that the behavior is not really a habit at all. Get help when you and your child need it.

Habits I Want My Child To Develop

List at least 10 habits that you want to see your child perform without being asked. Think of how you can start modeling those now, even before he's old enough to develop this habit. Get it firmly established in your own life right now.

1. _____

2. _____

3. _____

4. _____

5. _____

6. _____

7. _____

8. _____

9. _____

10. _____

Cultivating Habits You Want

Not all habits are bad habits. There is a host of small acts we'd like to have our kids do without even thinking:

- Saying "please," "thank you," and "excuse me"
- Closing the door when coming in from outside
- Putting toys away before leaving the room
- Fastening a seat belt without being asked
- Putting dirty dishes in the sink or the dishwasher

This is just a short list. Once you start thinking of good habits to cultivate, it seems there is no end to the fine things your kids could learn to do without being asked.

So how do you get started?

Of course, the first step in cultivating good habits is to model what you want to see. The old saying "Do as I say; don't do as I do" just doesn't hold much credibility. Actions do speak louder than words. Make good actions a habit for yourself first.

Then explicitly teach how and when to do what you'd like to see your child do. Take the time to put toys away before bed and demonstrate how this is done by actually participating. When you carry your snack plate to the kitchen, say what you're doing and why. If for some reason there's no time to do what should be done, let the child know. Say, "We should really pick up these toys, but Daddy's bus is coming and we don't want him to wait at the bus stop in the rain. We'll go now and clean up when we get back." Then remember to do what you said you would do.

It takes several weeks of consistent training for a habit to take hold. Remember to notice when your child finally does something you've been working on without being prompted. That is a day to celebrate.

Friends And Enemies
Helping your child get along

Getting Around

Having friends is an essential part of childhood. Since your child's peers are the people your child will live with all her life, it's important that she be able to get along with her age-mates, both in school and out. This means that it's important that you find friendship opportunities for your child while she's still small.

Sometimes parents are reluctant to let their children socialize with other kids. After all, it's hard enough to predict what your own child is going to do sometimes. What if another child hits or bites your child? What if your child picks up bad habits from a kid she meets?

Well, get over it. Children can't live in a bubble all their lives and sooner or later they all must learn to get along with other kids. And that means that you have to let your child learn by providing opportunities to hang out with other children and by not managing every encounter she has. While of course you won't put your child in danger and you will monitor your child's ventures out into the world, you do need to let your kid get around. Gradually, over the first four years, your child needs to learn how to manage her own affairs with her peers.

It's not enough to get along with siblings, if your child has siblings. It's not enough to get along with cousins or just the one child next door. Building a socially savvy and confident kid starts early. You can help.

Friends Over Time

How do self-centered babies become peer-oriented teens? Here's how.

Infants find other infants interesting but don't play with them.

Toddlers engage in "parallel play." They enjoy playing beside other toddlers but don't really play with them.

Preschoolers can play together, though they still have trouble sharing or planning cooperative play.

Kindergarteners can engage in imaginative play together, where roles are plotted ("You be the mommy and I'll be the baby") and a story line is followed.

Game play can start as early as age three, with Hide and Seek. Board games can be played by four-year-olds and become more and more important as kids grow older.

Friends' opinions increase in importance during kids' elementary school years. Children gradually shift their focus from their mom and dad to their peers.

Middle school kids still enjoy doing things with their parents but value their time with their friends equally.

High school kids value their time with their friends more than they value time with their mom and dad. Teenage boys seem to play more than teenage girls. They use video game play, sports, and rough-housing as a way to interact with peers.

The Roots Of Friendliness

The older the child, the wider the social circle and the more freedom needed to manage his own interactions. Babies under two years old enjoy being with other babies, but they don't establish relationships like older kids do. So occasional interactions with cousins or the babies of family friends is enough.

Two- and three-year-olds are able to establish links to children they see consistently. While these might not be actual friendships at age two, by age three they are. Even children this small can become quite attached to each other. By the end of age three, children will be able to be nice to each other a lot of the time.

By four years old, children can establish friendships and they can have enemies too, or at least kids they want to avoid. So they need to have some strategies to cope with kids who make them nervous. Four-year-old kids do well in groups away from home with another adult than their parent in charge. It's a good idea to give your child this experience before he starts kindergarten.

By kindergarten, kids should have enough social experience under their belts that they can introduce themselves to others, organize play with others, manage conflicts, and accept a playmate's occasional rudeness or mean behavior without completely falling apart. The kindergartener should have a sense of fairness, should be able to stand up for himself without resorting to violence, and should be able to resist temptation to follow the crowd at least some of the time.

To learn all this in only five short years is remarkable. Practice makes perfect.

Are You Shy?

Experts suggest that parents model outgoing behavior so kids can see how a person introduces himself to someone new, finds a place for himself in a group, and strikes up a conversation. Do you do those things?

I enjoy new social situations.
Yes   Sometimes   No

I find it easy to make new friends.
Yes   Sometimes   No

I usually say "Hello" to people I meet on the street.
Yes   Sometimes   No

I can strike up a conversation with strangers.
Yes   Sometimes   No

I have made more than 12 new friends this past year.
Yes   Sometimes   No

I don't mind going to an event by myself.
Yes   Sometimes   No

I don't believe I'm shy.
Yes   Sometimes   No

Helping The Shy Child

Sometimes you're ready for your child to venture forth into kid society but she has trouble making a move. She may be just naturally slow to warm up. There's nothing wrong with that. But if in addition to being reserved your child is also *unsure* of herself, then she needs some help to become more confident. Reserved but confident people are respected. Shy and uncertain people get only pity.

Shy children are often afraid of having their boundaries infringed upon. So your task as a parent is to help your child accept others' interest while still maintaining his distance.

Two steps will help you. First, provide your child with a scripted response he can use in the most common situations he will face. He can be guided to nod his head and say "Hi" or "Hello" when meeting adults. He can practice saying "My name is...." when asked. Low-key, supportive practice at home will go a long way to boosting his confidence when he needs to respond to strangers.

Second, ease the way in social situations by introducing your child instead of making her wait for a cue. Say, "Good morning, Hank. This is my daughter Clara." Then proceed to the rest of your conversation with Hank. At the same time, don't permit the stranger to chase your child with questions. Permit her to answer but then take control of the conversation and turn the spotlight away from her. As she becomes more capable, certainly let her carry on as long as she wishes, but protect her from discomfort.

In addition, be careful to not label your child. Labels have a way of sticking. So don't make the excuse, "Toby is shy." And don't fret with your child in public or laugh at him in your own nervousness. Be part of the solution.

More Self-Control

Remember that children are self-centered. They interrupt adults not because they're rude, but because they don't really notice you're talking to someone. They also don't have very well-developed memories. They know that if they don't tell you this *now*, they'll forget it.

The show-off is hungry for attention. He can't think of a way to join the conversation, so he "performs" instead.

To help your child develop self-control, invite him into the conversation.

"John, I'm talking to Mr. Wallace right now. Please wait one minute."

or

"John, we're talking about your school. Tell us what you like best about your class."

A friendly arm around the shoulder can sometimes calm things down. If self-control is a continuing problem for your child, then it's something you'll need to work on every day. Practice will eventually make perfect.

Helping The Excitable Child

Some children react to new situations by turtle-ing into their shells. But others react by talking full-tilt, showing off, and running around out of control. Both the shy child and the excitable child simply don't know what else to do. Just as you would help the shy child manage social situations, you need to help an excitable child too.

So instead of waiting for the next instance where your child runs amok with a new acquaintance and then yelling or holding him to get him back under control, practice ahead of time. Think of this as acting class. Teach your child how to take on the role of someone who has dignity and self-control. Plan ahead of time what three things he can tell a stranger he is introduced to: his name, how old he is, and one thing he did that day or is doing now ("Hi. I'm Paul, and I'm four. We're going to get a balloon.") Practice with your child how to introduce himself to another child on the playground and invite her to play.

Then find opportunities to practice. The excitable child can be a handful sometimes, but more practice, not less, is helpful. Give positive feedback as soon as you can after meeting someone, and review what to say and do if more work is needed. Practice. Practice. Practice.

Before going someplace new (out to a restaurant for dinner, for example) go over what will happen and what is expected. Script the most likely interactions (ordering a meal) and practice speaking in a quiet voice. Your child doesn't realize how she is coming across or that she's talking at the top of her voice. Practice speaking with control.

And be careful not to label your child. She's not being "hyper." Making her think she is only cements the behavior in both your minds. She's fine. She just needs guidance.

How Do You Get Your Way?

Everyone gets angry. How you express anger has a lot to do with how your parents expressed their anger. But you learned how to get your own way through your other relationships too.

What do you do to get your way? Write that here.

How can you *model* what you want *your kids* to do?

Biting And Hitting

At the 2008 Summer Olympic Games in Beijing, a boxer was disqualified after he bit his opponent on the shoulder. In the audience was American boxer Evander Holyfield who was bitten on the ear by opponent Mike Tyson during a match in 1997.

Grown men biting each other is news. Two-year-olds biting each other is not. But the impulse is the same: when you're not getting what you want and there's no way to get it in a civilized way (or when you forget all civility), then biting is pretty effective. It gets people's attention. Hitting works too but requires some coordination and force (which even professional boxers might feel they don't have enough of). Little kids hit and bite when they can't think of anything else to do to get their way and when they don't have the verbal ability to express their anger effectively.

But when children older than two still bite to make a point, that's a problem. Kids older than three who hit as their first or second approach to problem solving also need some help to "use your words." Take some time to teach stopping and thinking before acting. Teach what to say to an opponent ("I don't like what you did") and even practice telling the teacher what happened. Talk about the value of walking away.

In addition, be certain that you model non-violent problem-solving yourself. Never hit your child. And be careful about teaching a child to fight back. We'll talk about that more in a bit, but small children aren't very reliable in assessing threats. They may "hit back" in situations where that's an escalation of aggression, not a response to it. Hitting and biting will get your kid into trouble. Help him to find alternate ways to assert himself.

Stopping A Bully In His Tracks

Bullies pick on easy targets. Help your child avoid being targeted by making these suggestions.

1. Avoid being around the bully if you can. If you have to be where the bully is, have your own friends with you.
2. Ignore the bully as a first response. Practice appearing unconcerned and unimpressed.
3. Develop your own self-confidence. The more sure you can be that the bully can't hurt you, the less likely you'll be a target for a bully.

If your child is targeted, then he should:
1. Get away. Run to where there are other people.
2. If you can't get away, fight back *hard*.
3. Don't keep your encounters secret. Tell an adult.

Remind your child that being bullied is not his fault, and bullies will be punished in the end. What bullies do is wrong. Your child may not be sure of this. It's not uncommon for kids to feel like they somehow deserve to be targeted. Make sure your kid doesn't feel this way.

The Bully

Intimidation is an interaction style. It's not very nice and it's unattractive in adults as well as in children. But some people feel it works for them. Check and see if you're one of those people.

Because most kids who bully other kids have been bullied themselves, they have experienced first-hand what it feels like to be dominated and manipulated. They know how effective it can be.

Bullying can be physical. Kids can waylay others on the school bus or in the playground, hit them, take their lunch money, and shove them around. But bullying can also be verbal or psychological. It's bullying to spread lies about somebody, to blackmail someone, and to withhold friendship until a person agrees to do ridiculous things.

Bullies are successful because it seems easier to comply with their demands than to confront them. In fact, it can be dangerous to take on a bully alone. Even small children realize that bullies just don't have the same moral sense that other kids do. It's not possible to tell what a bully might do next if she doesn't get her way the first time. Bullies gather supporters through intimidation. This makes it easy to think that "everyone" agrees with the bully and that she must be right about her victim.

So if your child is being bullied, he needs adult support and intervention. Your child needs to know that the bully is wrong and to have confidence in his own perception of the situation. And your child needs strategies for how to respond to a bully's actions.

It's important that you take a child's complaint about being bullied seriously. Your quick response can make your child more confident and nip bullying before it takes over.

Your Friendship Attitudes

How good a friend are you? Since children learn by watching their parents, see if you're setting a good example for friendliness.

Do you know the first names of both your next-door neighbors and also the people who live across the street (or across the hall)? Write their names here.

Have you helped a neighbor with something in the past month? Write what you did here.

Have you refused a neighbor's request for help or if you had to refuse, did you offer an alternative solution to the problem? Write about that here.

Do you wave or speak to people you pass on your street, even if you don't know them personally?

No Friends?

Having no friends is no fun.

Like many childhood difficulties, your anxiety over your child's friendlessness can do more harm than good. So try not to make a big deal of this. But behind the scenes figure out what's going on.

Are there kids around to be friends with? If it's miles to the next house you might have to arrange play dates and outings with children from school or your church group.

Are there kids around, but your child doesn't like any of them, or none of them like your child? Figure out why this is. Be a quiet observer and see if the problem is:

- *The neighborhood kids are controlled by a bully and your child won't go along with the pack.* If you can influence the bully, try that. But you may have to arrange play dates with distant children as if there were no kids nearby.

- *The neighborhood kids are okay but your child can't figure out how to play with them.* Some kids lack "pragmatic skills" and have trouble picking up cues from others. Your child might be awkward around other kids. If so, you will have to help him practice playing with others and introducing himself. He might find it easier to practice with younger children.

- *The neighborhood kids are okay but they just won't do what your child wants them to.* She gets frustrated and quits playing. Your child may need some help in sharing and cooperating. And she may feel like she's not getting enough freedom at home and so needs to boss others around. Lighten up at home and help her to play nice.

Children who have no friends have a hard time in school. It's important that you help your child make connections.

10 Tips For Helping Kids Be More Inclusive

1. Enroll your child in a school with a diverse community of kids.

2. Live in a neighborhood that includes different kinds of people and family configurations.

3. Invite everyone in your child's class to birthday parties and give a Valentine to everyone in the class, not just to some.

4. At the playground, encourage your child to play with whoever is there.

5. Teach your child to share his toys.

6. Invite different children to your home for play dates.

7. Encourage a cooperative spirit instead of competition.

8. Travel with your kids, even if it's just to other neighborhoods in your own city. Get out and see more people.

9. Take public transportation.

10. Speak well of other people. Model attitudes you want to see in your child.

Including Everyone

In her 1993 book, *You Can't Say You Can't Play,* teacher Vivian Paley describes her attempt to enforce the rule in her kindergarten classroom that anyone who asks to play with someone else must be included. Kids were so upset by this rule that Dr. Paley surveyed the rest of the school: What did older kids think? She found that although older kids understood the plight of children who were rejected as playmates, they nonetheless agreed with the kindergarteners that everyone has the right to decide who can play with them and who cannot.

And that is indeed the problem. Some children are rejected by their peers. Children who do the rejecting often are not trying to be mean. They are simply asserting their right to play with children whom they like.

At first glance, this seems to be the American way of thinking. What can be wrong with having the freedom to choose one's friends? But the problem is not choosing friends but rejecting others. Learning how to play and get along with people is the central task of your child's early life. His ability to develop his social skills is stunted if he is allowed to play only with people he always gets along with. Your own child (the one who wants to reject someone else) is damaged as much as the child who is rejected.

So being inclusive, as Dr. Paley tried to require, is not only the compassionate and socially responsible course, it is selfishly good practice too. Encourage your child to be kind and friendly and teach her to get along as best she can with all sorts of people. She will be more successful in life with this early development of social skills.

Building Social Skills

The friendless child may need help in these areas:

- How to strike up a conversation and keep the conversation going with other kids.

- How to listen to someone else.

- What sorts of things other kids are interested in. Your child may be fascinated by fire trucks, but if other kids his age are interested in dinosaurs or NASCAR, then help him develop those interests too.

- How to engage in physical play. Help your child feel confident playing kickball or Twister. Get your kid moving more and she'll feel more confident.

- How to speak loudly enough to be heard.

- How to pick up on jokes and verbal silliness.

Work on these skills with your child every day and make sure she has opportunities to practice. It doesn't help, though, to try to convince other kids to help your child be accepted. No one picks a friend because her mother wants it. Your child has to build her friendship skills so she can be an attractive friend all on her own.

Fitting In

Children who are rejected are somehow different from the others. Rejected kids tend to be more aggressive or more shy than other kids, less able to pick up play cues from others, or have a neglected appearance. If kids have been taught to be biased concerning race or gender, those can be rejected qualities too.

Rejection matters because it becomes a way of life. Preschoolers who are rejected become elementary school students who are rejected and become high school students who never fit in. Rejection is linked with poor school performance, depression, and violent acting-out.

If you are the parent of a rejected child, what other kids do is beyond your control. Trying to get other kids to change won't convince them. You must focus instead on your own child. How can you help her fit in?

First decide if the peer group she's in is compatible with her interests and values. If the kids around her are kids you'd like her to be friends with, then great. But if the kids around her are as different from your child as people from another planet, then first you have to find a more compatible group. There's no point trying to fit in where she already feels uncomfortable. So find one.

Once you've got the right set of peers, then pretend that your child has just moved to the neighborhood. Start a play group, invite someone to go with you to the zoo, involve your child in a sports team or other activity. Consider what it is that makes your child different from other kids and teach ways around those differences.

And help your child to recognize that she is worthy and valuable no matter how many friends she has.

Hitting Back

If you're a person who wants his kid to retaliate for every offense, take a moment to think about how this has worked for you in your life. Can you answer, "That's true" to each of these questions?

Retaliation has never got me into any trouble.

People like me more because I retaliate.

Retaliation always defuses the situation.

I can use my impulse to retaliate at work, at home, and in the neighborhood with no problem.

Retaliation has enhanced my reputation as a respectable person.

I object to violence because when it appears to do good, the good is only temporary; the evil it does is permanent.
—Indian statesman Mahatma Ghandi

The Art Of Self-Defense

I know what you're thinking. All this fitting in and letting others play and being nice to people is fine and well if the kids in your neighborhood try to do all that too. But what if the kids in your neighborhood are not all that nice? Am I suggesting that you teach your child to let others walk all over him?

No.

Every child should know what his own boundaries are and should feel empowered to defend them. Not physical boundaries—I don't mean your child should guard your backyard like a pit bull. I mean moral and ethical boundaries. Every child should be confident of what physical contact he permits from others, what actions he will agree to do, and, more importantly, what he will *not* permit and what he will *not* do. The child who has no personal boundaries and who permits others to do to him whatever they please is a danger to himself.

But once your child is confident of her boundaries she also needs to be confident of her ability to defend them. This might mean knowing some strategies to defuse a confrontation or how to hit back effectively or where to run for help. You will know best what your neighborhood situation requires your child to know. You will need to teach not only what to do and how but also *when*. You want your child to be able to defend herself without becoming a bully.

Martial arts instruction can be helpful. Choose a center that emphasizes self-discipline and control along with ways to master an opponent. The confidence that comes from self-control will help your child avoid being a target for others. Kids who are picked on tend to be kids who signal their lack of confidence. A confident kid is a safer child.

Knowing Right And Wrong
Building a conscience

Fairness And Feelings

We are all born egoists. A newborn is unable to notice that others are real people and is also unable even to notice that she herself is a real person. Without even self-awareness, it's not possible to be aware of others.

This changes over the first year and a half. By the time a child is toddling around she is able to notice the emotions of others and to respond to them. Your baby will be sad if you're sad, and she will try to comfort you. Your baby will begin to identify her own feelings and know the words for them. It is a milestone when a child recognizes that he is tired or frustrated and can tell you so.

As children grow in their ability to identify their own feelings and to notice that others have feelings too, they are more aware of what causes particular emotions. They understand that how we treat each other influences how we feel.

Children as young as two value kind treatment and know that when they are unkind others get angry or sad. They know that when they are kind others are happier. They still have trouble acting on this knowledge (kids this age are still ego-centered) but it's comforting to know that the impulse to behave compassionately and fairly appears to be hard-wired into the human species. We all are predisposed to get along.

So developing your child's conscience is not something you have to do from scratch. You just have to nurture what is already there.

Theory Of Mind

One way researchers test for theory of mind is with this interesting experiment.

Two children are in a room. A researcher opens a box to show both children that the box contains candy. One of the children is then sent out of the room.

While the second child watches, the researcher empties the candy from the box and replaces it with pencils. He then asks the child, "When your friend comes back in the room, what will he think is in the box?"

The child who has developed a theory of mind will answer, "Candy." This child can imagine that the first child still holds in mind the original contents of the box and doesn't know that the candy has been replaced.

The child who hasn't developed a theory of mind will answer, "Pencils." This child knows that pencils are now in the box and can't realize that the child who is out of the room doesn't know about the switch.

Theory of mind usually develops between ages four and seven.

Intentionality

Over the preschool years, children gradually develop the idea that other people think their own thoughts. This is called developing a "theory of mind" and it's a key step in knowing right from wrong. For one thing, once a child understands that others have thoughts of their own, she can understand that others might cause things to happen on purpose or that things can happen just by accident.

The ego-centered child who hasn't developed a theory of mind believes that whatever you do you intended to do. If you accidentally bump into her, she believes you meant to do it and is naturally upset with you. The child who has developed a theory of mind understands that what you were thinking at the time you hit her matters. If you intended to hit her then she is justified in feeling upset. But if you hit her by accident then she realizes she was not treated unfairly.

Being able to tell right from wrong involves this ability to determine our own intentions and the intentions of others. Accidents carry little moral weight. Unless we contributed to the accident by our negligence, things that happen by accident are not our fault. But if we intended a bad thing to happen to someone else, then it was our fault and we should feel guilty. Preschoolers understand this. They often bop someone over the head then claim it "was an accident."

A theory of mind develops as a child's brain develops and there's not much you need to do to make it happen quicker. But once your child seems to understand that others can have purposes of their own, you can reinforce the moral difference between intentional acts and accidents. Be careful not to punish your child for what was clearly an accident. And point out to your young child that meaning to hurt someone makes the action punishable. Intention counts.

"Why Did You Tell Me It Was True?"

A kindergartener asked his dad how Santa Claus watches children and knows what they want for Christmas. After a bit of dithering, Dad said, "Do you want the fun answer or the real answer?" His son said, "The real answer, of course!"

So Dad explained about Santa Claus. After a shocked silence, his son asked, "Why did you ever tell me Santa Claus was true?"

Whatever you think about Santa Claus, this story points out how ingrained in our culture it is to tell people something other than the truth. If you find it hard to say that telling a child about Santa Claus or the Tooth Fairy is *lying*, that just demonstrates that we find ways to sugar-coat our fibbing. We all know lying is wrong. So we don't call what we do lying. We call it "fun."

The young boy decided after a few days that Santa Claus is real after all, despite what his dad told him. Self-deceit happens too.

Why Kids Lie

Children can't lie until they develop a theory of mind: until they understand that each person's thoughts are private, and no one knows what someone else knows until that person tells him. So being able to lie is a developmental milestone that signals your child's intellectual growth. Isn't that nice?

And little kids—three- and four-year-olds—seem to actively test this out by telling you nonsense just to see if you'll believe it. This is good fun. Fibbing becomes more interesting when it's used to disguise the truth and mislead the listener. The question for us is why kids might do that.

Theory of mind develops right along with an understanding of right and wrong and the ability to feel guilt and shame. Guilt and shame are uncomfortable emotions most of us want to avoid. When guilt is accompanied by punishment we want to avoid admitting guilt even more. So lying is a natural reaction to wanting to avoid punishment and feeling guilty and ashamed.

Studies show that everyone lies. So we shouldn't be shocked when our kids lie. Lying becomes a problem when a person lies about everything so that his credibility about even trivial stuff is suspect. You want to help your child avoid using lying as a conversational technique.

You can minimize lying in two ways. First, never try to catch your child in a lie. If you know the truth, don't ask about the incident and provide an opportunity to lie about it. Just say what you know. And second, make telling the truth unpunishable. If your child freely admits to breaking a vase then don't punish her for breaking it. Thank her for being brave enough to tell the truth and clean up the broken bits.

Were You Ever Tempted?

Did you ever take something that didn't belong to you? What do you remember about that experience?

What did you take and what was your motivation at the time? What happened next? Did anyone find out? Did you return the item or pay for it?

How do you feel now about the experience?

Write about this here.

Why Kids Steal

Small children take things because they don't know it's wrong to do that. They see something. They want it. They put it in their pocket. Slightly older kids might take things simply to confirm the rules. A child might pocket a trinket off your desk, even let you know he's taken it, just to see what reaction this gets. He's really asking you to tell him that stealing is wrong.

Young kids also may take things simply because their ability to think before they act is not fully developed. They know they shouldn't have taken what they did, but they just didn't think about it at the time.

None of this is much cause for concern because the stealing is not really intentional. Your reaction should make clear that stealing is not tolerated and that whatever was taken has to be put back. Of greater concern is stealing that is deliberate.

Kids steal intentionally for one of several reasons. Children without much self-esteem can equate having things with being a worthy person. So kids might steal a cool-looking backpack or a team logo jersey in order to be accepted by a group of friends that has those things or simply to satisfy their own egos with trendy stuff.

Kids sometimes steal for revenge, to get back at a kid or a store-owner they think treated them unfairly. Kids can steal just because they feel life is stacked against them and stealing is a way to level the playing field. Finally, older kids sometimes steal on a dare or just to see if they can get away with it.

It's important that you figure out why your child steals. Use this event to reinforce your family's values. And use this event to help your child deal with the needs and pressures that she expresses by stealing.

What Happened Next?

Describe an incident between your child and you that required an apology. Tell what happened next and where things stand right now. If you can describe a second incident and its outcome, do that too.

The Incident I Thought of First

The Second Incident and How That Came Out

Apologies

"Say you're sorry."

Often this demand gets a sullen, head-down "Sorry" that just doesn't seem very sincere. The whole point of making an apology is to smooth over a problem and to re-learn how you should've behaved to begin with. If children apologize just by mumbling, "I'm sorry," nothing is gained. Worse, the child may come to think that any misbehavior can be solved with minimal effort on his part.

So making a good apology is an important part of what you teach your child about right and wrong. As with most things, kids will learn how to apologize best from watching you. So follow these guidelines when you apologize to your kids or to other people, and teach your kids to follow your example.

A good apology is made this way:
1. Make eye contact with the person you're apologizing to.
2. Include what you are apologizing for. Say, "I'm sorry I broke your toy."
3. Apologize for what you did, not for what the person you offended did. Don't say, "I'm sorry you got upset," since that means you're not really sorry for what you did but for the reaction it got.
4. If you want, explain how you made your mistake, but keep it short and keep it centered on your own error. You could say, "I should've been more careful" but not, "You should've put it further back on the shelf."
5. Don't demand forgiveness. Forgiveness is a gift, not a social nicety. It's not right for you to require that she say, "That's okay" or "I forgive you."

The ability to make a good apology is a key skill. Since we all make mistakes, you'll want to remember to teach it.

Family Rules

List the rules you think are important for your children to follow. After each, imagine a situation where you'd want your child to ignore the rule and follow his instincts.

1.

2.

3.

4.

5.

6.

7.

8.

9.

10.

Following The Rules

Young children believe rules are made to be followed because adults say so or because kids want to be good. This is a fine starting point. So begin by honoring rules and social conventions. Teach your child to follow the rules and to be trustworthy and courteous.

But by the time a child is seven or eight years old, you want him to understand why a particular rule is important and when it might be okay to break it. You want your child to be thoughtful about his behavior, not just obedient. You want your child to have a set of core values that are more important to him than rules. Your child will be out in the world without you, and you want him to be able to judge fair and reasonable rules from unfair and dangerous ones. Older kids who go along with risky games and law breaking are kids who never learned to trust their gut instead of going along with what others say they should do.

So blind obedience isn't your objective. Along with respect for rules and laws, you also want your child to have a sense of fairness and even wisdom. You want your child to be able to recognize injustice and fight against it even if he must challenge "the rules."

For your child to acquire this wisdom, you can't use the phrase "because I said so" as your justification for your own rules. A reason must exist for household rules, and the rules must be consistent from day to day and for everyone in the family. Your rules have to be fair. And both you and your child have to know why those rules are important.

Developing The Uh-Oh Sensor

Child safety educator and consultant Kim Estes of P.E.A.C.E. of Mind in Bellevue, Washington suggests that you teach your child to recognize the funny feeling that means, "This is scary." Estes calls this the "uh-oh feeling."

We all get that sudden clutching feeling in the stomach when something scary happens. It's a feeling that is hard-wired into our brains. The trick is to teach children what it means when they get that feeling. This is the reality of "trusting your gut."

Estes suggests looking for teachable moments. "When you're driving somewhere with your child and you have to stop suddenly to avoid hitting someone, that's a teachable moment," Estes says. "You can say something like "Wow, that was scary. It made me feel funny in my stomach. Did it make you feel like that?'"

Teach your child that a funny feeling means, "Uh-oh, I better watch out. Something bad is going to happen." Once your child understands how to interpret what his body is telling him, he will notice situations that look okay on the surface but are treacherous underneath.

Estes says, "The more open parents are about identifying and talking about their own "uh-oh" feelings the more kids know that everyone, even Mom and Dad, gets the "uh-oh" feeling and that it's okay to talk about it."

The subconscious mind knows. It picks up signals the conscious mind overlooks. It signals danger with that "uh-oh feeling." You want your child to know what that means and what to do.

Safe In An Unsafe World

No one has a better imagination than a parent. We can think of more unlikely disasters that can befall our children than anybody else.

The truth of the matter is, though, that you're likely to miss worrying about the one challenge your kid will face. You warn your son about strangers with lost puppies, but he encounters someone he knows who invites him home to watch videos. You warn your daughter about the bad part of town, but she runs into trouble right on your block.

Research shows that everyone imagines that danger is located in unfamiliar places and is perpetrated by people we don't know. But the facts are quite different. Most accidents and incidents occur in our own territory and involve individuals we know pretty well and had no concern about. So is the solution to warn children to distrust even people they see every day? Do we want our kids to be scared to step out the front door?

Obviously, no.

But it's important that we warn kids not about "strangers" but about people who act strangely and make strange requests. We need to arm our kids against any situation that is not quite right, even if it happens right there at home or at school. Evil-doers are good at staying under cover. You will not always be able to pick them out. And you won't be around when a bad-person-in-disguise finally shows her true self. Your child needs to know what to do.

So take the time to talk with your child about dangerous situations and what to do if she ever finds herself in one. Teach her to trust her gut. And respect her efforts to act on her instincts. She'll make some errors but with your support she'll feel (and be) safer.

Who Has Your Respect?

Think of people you know and respect. Then answer these questions:

Who always acts with integrity?

Whom do you trust?

How do these people act in their daily lives?

What about how they conduct themselves could you also do and teach to your children?

Respect

It all comes down to respect. Knowing right and wrong will be easy when your child respects her own rights and feelings and the rights and feelings of everyone else. It's that easy. And it's that hard.

In order to respect herself and be able to stand up for what she knows is right, your child must feel respected by you. This is your work in the first several years of life: to develop in your child her sense of self-worth and integrity. If you insult and belittle your child (or permit others to) and if you over-control her and make her think she doesn't know her own mind (or permit others to) then she will learn to distrust herself. She will be unable to withstand the power of powerful others.

In order to respect the rights of others, your child must first value other people as worthy human beings. "Other people" include folks you disapprove of and disagree with, as well as people like yourself. Now is the time to dial down your prejudices and biases and recognize that everyone is worthy of respect. Model the respect for others that is so important to develop in your child. The child who respects other people is someone who will resist the temptation to hurt them.

We are all tempted to hurt other people, in the mean words we might say, in the mean looks we could deliver, and in acts of violence and disregard we could inflict. Your child has these feelings too. What keeps you and your child from acting on these nasty impulses is your self-respect and sense of who you are and also your respect for others and for the good of society. Cultivate respect. It is the key to acting with moral authority.

The Glowing Eye
Television and other media

How Bad Is Television?

Communist philosopher Karl Marx called religion "the opiate of the masses." I can't tell if Marx was right about religion but I can say for sure that if Marx were alive today he would be more concerned about television. If ever there were a device that dulls the intellect and creates dependency, it's the black box in the family room.

So, yes, television is bad. It's estimated that the average preschooler watches over seven hours of television every week. But television is not just the daily companion of small people who can't yet read or volunteer in their communities. Adults watch an average of 21 hours of TV each week and older adults watch even more.

The problem with television is not the programs themselves (though, as we'll see next, those aren't exactly good). No, the problem for all of us is that television viewing takes away time we could have used to do other, more useful, educational, or inspiring things. As author Annie Dillard said, "How we spend our days is, of course, how we spend our lives." Too many of us spend "the days of our lives" in front of what Marshal McLuhan called "the idiot box."

So we all need to limit television viewing. We must shake off our own addiction and return television to its rightful place as an occasional source of entertainment or information. It has too long been instead our drug of choice.

Keep A TV Log

What did your family watch this week? Are you okay with the choices made and the time devoted to TV?

Monday

Tuesday

Wednesday

Thursday

Friday

Saturday

Sunday

What You Watch Does Matter

Ask most people how much TV they watch and you'll find they are quick to defend their viewing time by describing the value of the programs they watch. They'll tell you they "only watch the news" or follow a sports team or keep up with what their colleagues watch so they can fit in at work. Programming designed expressly for children adopts this rationale, too, by emphasizing how "educational" it is. Gone are the children's programs of the past that aspired to be merely entertaining.

But we fool ourselves, both about the value of what we watch and about what we actually do watch. Keep track of your viewing for a week and see just how necessary any of that is. And remember that even the news, programming on The Weather Channel, sports presentations, and news magazines choose what is broadcast by its *entertainment* value.

So given the fact that what we have to choose from on television is all entertainment programming, we have a responsibility to decide how we and our children will be entertained. What do you do want to permit in your living room? What ways of behaving and talking to other people do you want to have modeled for your kids? It doesn't matter if it's the nightly news or PBS or the movie channel. Decide what's appropriate for your family.

We know that children (and adults) do copy what they see on TV. For children especially, television teaches even when it's not intentionally educational. Violent, loud, rude, sexually explicit, and exploitative programs do contribute to real-life bad behavior. If these are the programs aired in your home, then expect difficulties to follow.

Television By The Numbers

While cutting out television altogether may be a losing proposition, cutting back on television is an excellent idea. Here are some shocking statistics.

43% of four- to six-year-olds have a television in their bedroom. The number rises to 69% of eight- to ten-year-olds.

Children who have a TV in their bedrooms do less well in school than kids who do not.

Children as young as two years old watch over an hour of TV per day, on average. Eight- to fourteen-year-olds watch over three hours every day. When you add in time spent in watching movies the numbers rise to an hour-and-a-half for two-year-olds and over four hours for older kids.

70% of child care centers use television during the day.

The average child sees 3,000 television ads per day.

Televised violence is copied by children. Children are disturbed by violent behavior on TV and may act it out as a way of dealing with it.

The more television kids watch, the more likely they are to be overweight. Decreasing the number of hours of television viewing every day results in lower body mass index in children and a more normal rate of weight gain.

The Problem With "No TV"

Are you thinking that maybe the solution to television is no television at all? Actually, that's not my first choice.

Television (and include also here movies and DVDs) is so much a part of American culture that it cannot be escaped. In fact, television *is* American culture: it reflects American culture like a mirror. We may not like what we see in the mirror but putting a towel over the glass doesn't change how we look. Trying to eliminate television from children's lives is like trying to eliminate American culture. It can be done, but at the cost of isolating children from the rest of kid society.

As we've seen, feeling isolated and rejected leads to other problems. In order to fit in with their peers, most kids will find ways at least to *pretend* they are knowledgeable about TV. Other kids will sneak behind their parents' backs to watch television. While not owning a television will naturally limit kids' television viewing, it will not eliminate it. In order to fit in, kids will find a way.

Limiting TV viewing to an arbitrary amount (like one program per week) has the effect of making television seem even more attractive than it is. Things that are scarce are valuable and even children understand this. By making television scarce, you enhance its importance.

So what's the answer? Certainly keep the TV turned off as much as you can, for yourself as well as for the kids. Watch television when it makes sense (because a particular program is interesting or because a child needs some calm time) not as part of the daily schedule. Avoid thinking that your child, or you, *must* watch a particular program every day or every week. Teach how to be a smart consumer of television. Use TV thoughtfully.

Video Game Ratings

The Entertainment Software Rating Board places indicators of age-appropriate content on video games. Remember though that "appropriate" doesn't mean "acceptable." As the parent, you still must decide if you want your child to play video games at all and if a particular game is acceptable.

Also, if your household includes older and younger kids, pay attention to what the older ones play that the younger ones may be exposed to.

Here are the ratings:

EC   Early Childhood. The content of these is appropriate for children ages three and older.

E   Everyone. The content is appropriate for children ages six and older. It includes mild violence and occasional mild bad language.

E 10+   Everyone Over 10. This content is appropriate for older kids and includes mild violence, mild bad language, and mildly suggestive themes.

T   Teen. The content here is intended for kids 13 and older. It includes violence, suggestive themes, strongly bad language, gambling, some blood, and crude humor.

M   Mature. This content is intended for kids 17 and older. It includes graphic violence, sexual themes, and strong language.

AO   Adults Only. Use your imagination and you'll come close to the content here.

Video Games Aren't All Bad

What is it about video games that drives some parents crazy? Is it the fantasy-world nature of video games? Is it the sometimes edgy or violent themes? Or is it their attractiveness for kids? Video games seem to be almost addictive.

Probably the answer is "all of the above." With today's video game rating system, parents can be fairly certain that the content of their kids' video games is not too mature for them. But the fact that video games are interactive—much more so than television—means that kids are *involved* in the action. Kids live video scenarios and the time-pressure and stress that seem part of even the tamest video games affect kids' emotional lives in a way that television usually does not.

The interactive quality of video games is what makes them habit-forming too. Game play is more fun and challenging than homework, school or doing chores around the house. Because video games seem "real," they can be more compelling than reading, even for good readers. So are video games bad?

Not really. Like any entertainment, video games shouldn't be allowed to be the only things kids do when they're home or an excuse for not doing other things. And like other entertainments (reading included), the maturity level and content of video games should be carefully monitored. But game play itself shapes the brain in 21st century ways that are even *advantageous* to today's kids.

Gamers develop spatial relations skills and their decision-making processes. They develop eye-hand coordination and an appreciation for visual imagery and storyline. These are important skills. As long as playing video games isn't the only thing your child does, playing occasionally is okay.

A Fuzzy Picture

An expert analysis by Future of Children presents a lukewarm view of computer use by children.

On the one hand, computers are very much here to stay and form an increasingly important part of adult communication and information-gathering. Children need computer skills to participate in all the good things computers bring to modern life. In fact, the lack of computers in some segments of American society is a cause for concern. The "digital divide" separates the haves and the have-nots.

Computer use by young children is small enough not to raise any red flags at this time. However, use by some older kids and teens is excessive. There is concern when hours of daily computer time replace physical and social activities that are important to most teens. The virtual world cannot substitute for the real world.

So, as with anything else, moderation and balance are important. Computer access at home is nearly a necessity to provide children with the tools for success. But just because something can be done on the computer doesn't mean it's done *best* on the computer. Sometimes, doing things "for real" is the way to go.

Across the world there is a passionate love affair between children and computers....They know they can master it more easily and more naturally than their parents. They know they are the computer generation.
—Seymour Papert, *The Connected Family*

Computers For Kids

Does your small child have an Internet presence right now? Is he featured on a website, are his pictures posted in a public spot somewhere, or does he star in a YouTube video? An astonishing number of infants and little kids are already public figures, thanks to their parents. That could be a problem.

Christopher Robin, the boy in the Winnie-the-Pooh stories, was the real son of the author. As an adult, he said he felt exploited. He wrote, "It seemed to me almost that my father had got where he was by climbing on my infant shoulders, that he had filched from me my good name and left me nothing but empty fame." Posting the details of your child's life is something you should do only with the greatest hesitation. This is not your life to share.

Which leads us to the more common complaint about kids' relationship to computers: that computers are dangerous portals to pornography, exploitation, and bad ideas. They certainly are. At the same time, computers are marvelous tools for thinking and creative expression. We don't want to throw the baby out with the bath water. We don't want to restrict computer use by kids in order to protect them. We do want to guide kids' computer use to nurture them.

Every older child needs to be skilled in using computers and the Internet. But adult guidance is important. And make sure the computer your child uses is never used to visit adult-only sites. Once those are in your machine's history, your child can stumble upon those sites without meaning to. Teach safe surfing but model it too.

And begin by keeping your child's face and stories to yourself, sharing them only with friends and family. Don't set your child up for exploitation by being the first to exploit your child.

Online Education

Teaching and learning online are quite different from teaching and learning in a classroom. As more high schools (and programs for even younger kids) move into online learning, it makes sense to take a closer look at those differences.

Online learning requires:

- Good reading skills, especially the ability to understand and follow written directions.

- Good writing skills. Everything online is written, so being a good writer is important.

- Good computer skills, including the ability to send and open email attachments, find websites, download files, and participate in chat rooms and discussion boards.

- A computer with a fast Internet connection and really good virus protection.

- An ability to work independently and manage time effectively.

- A good imagination. An online learner often has to fill in the gaps in online conversations.

- Decent social skills. People who enjoy online learning the most are the ones who are online a lot, making side conversations, talking about assignments, and so on.

Online learning may not be for everyone, but the skills it requires are important in today's world.

Kids And Online Communities

One source estimates that 20% of children who use the Internet are propositioned by an adult while online. Many of these children didn't realize that the person they were interacting with was a whole lot older than them.

Is the solution keeping your pre-teen and teen age children off the Internet? Should you close their MySpace accounts?

Well, let's not panic.

The truth is that online communities are here to stay and have a lot to offer. And social networking is such an important part of many kids' lives that any attempt to eliminate it will likely drive it underground where you'll be unable to influence it.

So a better course is to teach and re-teach all the stranger-danger stuff you teach your four-year-old. "Don't talk to strangers" is still a good idea, but older kids online need to know how to identify a dangerous stranger pretending to be just another kid. Older kids need to know what information is safe to share in a public space like an online forum. And kids need to know how to move safely from online conversation to in-person conversation over a Pepsi at the mall.

Besides knowledge, teens need self-esteem. The kid who feels needy and friendless is more likely to accept an online offer of companionship than the kid who is already busy with real-life relationships. We spoke earlier about the problems of kids who are socially out-of-step. Vulnerability online is yet another. Do what you can to get your kid involved in school activities, sports or other "real-life" communities.

The More Music The More Musical

Music is a good thing. While we know that playing classical music doesn't make a person smarter in the way the mythical The Mozart Effect promised, we do know that listening to music increases musical ability. So playing music or singing is a good thing to do and to encourage your children to do.

It doesn't have to be classical music. Whatever genre of music you like or your kids like is fine. Musical ability in that type of music will increase.

Music is a better choice when you want "background noise" than television. Television running all day just to fill up the silence actually interferes with children's vocabulary development. Music interferes with nothing.

So play music. Play what you like.

Learning to play an instrument is even better. People who play an instrument seem to have increased memory power. Their brains are different in ways that make complex movements easier and that link both sides of the brain more strongly. It seems likely that musical practice shapes musicians' brains in this way.

So whatever music you like and your children like, play it, and play or sing along. Enjoy.

Your Kids And Their Music

Did you know that the ballet *Rite of Spring* was considered so offensive when it first was performed in 1913 that there was rioting in the concert hall? Imagine gowned and tuxedoed adults hitting each other at the symphony. So if you don't like today's music join the club: it's nothing new. The question is what can you do about it? Is a riot in order?

Probably not. First, be reassured on a couple points. Research indicates that people who like particular sorts of music are *happi*er when they listen to that music, even if other people find the music annoying, depressing or disturbing. Second, research points out that kids do not pay attention to lyrics as much as adults do.

So take these factors into account if you talk to your kids about their music. First actually listen to the music yourself. Tell them what you find hard to take about it. Kids are often unaware of messages of sexual exploitation, bigotry, and hate that upset their parents. Ask your kids what they like about the music you hate.

If you decide to forbid the playing of some music at home (as you might especially if there are younger children there), understand that you won't be able to keep older teens from listening to this music at all. Be ready to negotiate with your teens. With younger kids you may want to exert more control, though your real power to limit listening might itself be limited. Remember that your protests will force your child to defend his choice and actually will make his loyalty to it stronger, rather than cause him to change his mind and agree with you.

And just as *Rite of Spring* became accepted by music lovers, your kids' music just might grow on you.

Were You Ever Bamboozled?

Did you ever purchase something you saw on television or that was pitched on the Internet and then found out it wasn't "as advertised"?

Recall how easy it was to be fooled and what you learned from that experience. What misleading ads can you think of that are running right now? How can you help your kids see past the hoopla and evaluate products and services intelligently?

Becoming A Wise Consumer

It comes down to this: media use is an opportunity for you to teach your children about making wise choices in what they put in their minds, in how they use their time and in how they interpret commercial messages and other lures. These are lessons that don't need to be absorbed all at once. You can teach them in small steps, with choices made every day, over the entire time of their childhoods.

Your task as a parent is to get your kids to the point of responsible adulthood. Knowing how to manage media is part of that. So make media use part of the discussion at home.

No discussion of media and consumerism, though, is complete without talking about commercials. It's estimated that the average kid sees 3,000 commercial messages every day. Kids recognize brands and company logos before they learn to read. It's no secret that companies target children in their ads even for products only adults might use (like car insurance) and for products it's illegal for children to use (like alcohol and cigarettes).

Children and even teenagers have a hard time distinguishing between what is perfectly true and what is only part of the truth. The idea that "it must be so because I read it on the Internet" and "it must be so because I saw it on TV" is well-established even among adults. In addition, commercials create desire and even *need* for things that are not really necessary and weren't even wanted before.

Helping your kids develop their flim-flam radar is a good thing to do. Knowing where the Off button is and when to use it helps too.

Going To School
Are we ready?

Is Preschool Necessary?

How important is it to send your four-year-old to preschool? If you're doing fine at home, should you still get her into some sort of group situation somewhere?

Well, let's see. Preschool provides opportunities for a young child to:
- get along with other children
- accept the authority of adults who aren't her parents
- follow directions
- attempt tasks and persist in completing them
- handle disappointment and manage conflict
- be independent of her parents
- learn how to be a friend
- make herself understood by others and
- be organized in managing tasks and materials.

These are essential skills. These are the skills children need to be successful in school (and in life).

Nowhere on this list are things like learning the alphabet or how to color within the lines. Academic activities like these are not nearly so important as social skills. Social skills are key.

So while it's possible to teach kids the alphabet and counting at home, it is far more difficult to teach the social skills that are really important. For that you need other kids and a teacher. For that you really do need preschool.

Sorting Out Preschool "Brands"

There are a lot of different philosophies when it comes to preschool education. Here are the features and things to watch for about some of these.

Academic
What it is: Heavy focus on school skills like reading
But watch for: Too little play or a too-stressful atmosphere

Cooperative
What it is: A traditional program with parents assisting
But watch for: Untrained parents who may cause conflict

Language-immersion
What it is: Most conversation done in a second language
But watch for: Slower mastery of a child's home language

Montessori
What it is: Highly individualized teaching of specific skills
But watch for: Too little imaginative play

Play-based
What it is: Children follow their interests in fulltime play
But watch for: Too little teacher direction in learning

Traditional
What it is: 1960s-style program with lots of teacher talk
But watch for: Low creativity and little diversity of ideas

Waldorf
What it is: Program based in arts and traditional stories
But watch for: Expectation of a restrictive family lifestyle

How To Choose The First School

Often parents choose a preschool by what's near home or on their way to work. Cost is another big factor. Private education at any grade level is expensive and you've got many expenses to cover. Relatively lower cost and a relatively more convenient location pretty much seal the selection of a preschool. You're also more likely to choose a preschool your friends recommend or that markets itself heavily.

But are these the best ways to make a wise choice? Here are some things to look for in choosing a preschool:

- Look first at how children are spoken to and how teachers respond to misbehavior and emotional upsets. You want to see calm teachers who treat children with respect and kindness.

- Observe the way the classroom is arranged. Is there lots of room to play? Is children's work displayed and is it not all the same? Is the room neat and orderly?

- Look at what children are doing. You want to see children working together without much teacher direction. You don't want to see children sitting and listening for long periods of time. Children learn by doing. Are they permitted to do things? Are the things they can do interesting?

- Remember also that parents should always be welcome at any time of day.

Most preschools are, if not excellent, then at least good enough. Finding these is not so difficult that parents shouldn't try. Choose the very best you can find for your kids.

What Kindergarten Teachers Want

Five-year-olds don't need to come to school "ready to read." They need to come to school ready to learn. Long-time kindergarten teacher Elisabeth Stambaugh says...

Kindergarten teachers are pleased if students can:
- Put on, fasten, unfasten and take off clothes, like coats, shoes and mittens
- Use the bathroom and wash their hands.
- Follow two- and three-step-directions. (An example of a two-step direction is "hang up your coat and come sit down.")
- Carry on a conversation, including staying on the subject.
- Get along with other kids and adults, by sharing, taking turns and avoiding fights.
- Stay on-task for a reasonable length of time.
- Accept the authority of the teacher and other school adults.

In addition, kindergarten teachers would love it if students come to school able to:
- Identify many upper and lower case letters of the alphabet and numerals to 10.
- Identify basic colors and shapes.
- Open a book, turn pages, interpret the action by observing pictures.
- Listen and understand a conversation.
- Use a pencil to draw a shape or figure, make a straight cut with a pair of scissors, and use glue or paste conservatively.
- Print their first names and recognize their first names in print.

When To Start Kindergarten

Most school districts around the country have a "cut-off date" for children beginning public kindergarten. In my city the date is September 1st. Kids who turn five before September 1st are eligible to start school that year but kids who turn five on or after that date wait for the next year.

However, in very few states are five-year-olds *required* to start kindergarten when they turn five. In my state, kids don't have to attend school until they're eight.

So this means that parents often have the option of deciding when to send their children to kindergarten. And there are some myths surrounding that.

Parents sometimes think that keeping an eligible five-year-old out of school for an extra year will help him do better in school since he'll be more able to sit still. And some parents think that holding a kid back will make him more successful in high school athletics, since he'll be bigger and stronger than other kids.

While each child is different, and it makes sense to start a child in kindergarten only when he's ready, it's important to remember a couple things. First, any class of kids already includes an entire year's worth of ages so the held-back child may not be at much of an advantage at all. And studies show that the most common characteristic of high school drop-outs is being older than classmates, no matter what the reason. So holding a child back may not be a good idea.

Early entrance can also be a problem. Parents sometimes want to start a child a year ahead if she's already reading at age three or four. But remember that kindergarten is about social skills. The child who is younger than her classmates will struggle with fitting in, and that puts her at a disadvantage.

Pluses And Minuses

Consider what you're looking forward to as your child starts the school year (whether it's his kindergarten year or another grade) and also what concerns you about the upcoming year. Just writing down your thoughts helps to sort them out and gives you a platform for thinking.

What I'm looking forward to for my child in school this year.

What concerns me about my child in school this year.

Your Role As A Kindergarten Parent

Starting "real school" can feel like a big step for both children and their moms and dads. For the first time, someone outside the family evaluates a child's progress. Parents quite naturally want their children to do well. There is value placed on kindergarten that was not part of preschool. This causes anxiety and stress.

So the first step to take in getting ready for kindergarten is to recognize that you might feel tense and anxious. Try to avoid getting all wound up over "the right" school clothes or the selection of "the right" teacher. Try to take a balanced view.

The second thing to remember is that school personnel are on the child's side. Teachers want your child to do well. So when teachers point out the difficulty a child is having with one school task or another, this isn't intended as criticism. It's information.

Finally, remember that you had your time in kindergarten, but this is your child's time. Don't try to take over the experience from your child or manage it for him. So while you certainly can help your child when he's stuck, don't do his homework. And don't insist he do things the way you want him to. Let your child own his school life. Recognize that in starting kindergarten, he is starting a part of his life that is separate from yours.

That is really the impact of kindergarten, for children and parents. Both realize that kindergarten is the start of the growing apart that must happen if kids are ever to become adults themselves. Granted, this is just the beginning and the process will take more than a decade to accomplish. But it's a scary step, and no one is ever ready. The best you can do, children and parents alike, is just to start.

241

Rate Your Involvement

Think about the last school year (or if your child isn't in school yet, remember your own parents' involvement when you were a kid). Add up the points in each ( ).

Number of parent-teacher conferences you attended:
None (0)   One (1)   All of them (2)

Number of parent-teacher conferences your child's other parent attended:
No (0)   Some (1)   All of them (2)

Number of times you volunteered at the school:
None (0)   Once (1)   Lots (2)

Number of times you attended a school event (like a play, art show, football game, pancake breakfast or whatever):
None (0)   Once (1)   Lots (2)

Number of times you called the principal to complain:
None (0)   Once (1)   Lots (-1)

Number of times you called the principal to give praise:
None (0)   Once (1)   Lots (2)

Number of times you called a teacher to complain:
None (0)   Once (1)   Lots (-1)

Number of times you called a teacher to ask about your child or to ask if you could help:
None (0)   Once (1)   Lots (2)

Your score: *11 to 14 – You're a real contributor*
6 to 10 – You're an involved parent
0 to 5 – You could do a lot more

Elementary School And Beyond

Kindergarten is only the tip of the iceberg. Throughout your child's school years, your task is to help your child stay focused on meeting classroom responsibilities, getting along with other kids and with teachers, and enjoying learning and being curious about things.

It's not your job to make sure your kid is a star. That's his job—or not. Have high expectations, provide the tools and materials he needs (within reason), and share moral support and strategies for getting things done. But don't do the work for him. Don't make his school success your project. Make being his parent your project.

Support your child's school and his teachers. Go to the school's fall open house and attend every parent-teacher conference. When you can, volunteer. Parent involvement in a child's school rubs off on the child. It's a consistent contributor to children's school success.

This doesn't mean you have to agree with the school on every point. But it does mean that when you disagree with a school decision, you work with the school to try to sort things out. Disrespect rubs off on your kid just as much as positive involvement does. Remember that your child's success in life as well as in school depends on his showing up, doing the work, and treating people well.

There will be ups and downs in your child's school career. Some years will be rugged and others will be loads of fun. It's all educational. Every piece of it strengthens your kid's coping skills, provides him with valuable life experience, and tests his resolve to discover and become his own true self.

And it does all that for parents too.

Should You Home School?

Parents choose homeschooling for many reasons. Before you do, keep these facts in mind:

- Homeschooling is legal in every state, but every state has rules about homeschooling. Check out the rules so you know what they are in your location.

- If you home school your child and then decide to send him to public school later, you probably won't have trouble doing that, though your child may need to be tested to determine his grade placement. Most colleges accept homeschooled students without a problem, provided they meet other entrance requirements.

- Teaching is a full-time occupation so to do homeschooling well you will need to treat this like a full-time job. Good teaching is more than just assigning worksheets and reading from a book. Unless you want your child to get a lousy education, you will have to become a really fine teacher.

- A child's school experience includes more than academics. Kids learn how to get along with others, how to work well in groups, how to interact with different authority figures, and how to manage their time. If you home school your child, realize that he will miss out on these skills unless you find ways to meet them.

- If you ask a child what he likes about school, he will mention his friends in the first few sentences. School is where your child's peers are. If your child doesn't go to school, you will have to find ways for him to connect with other kids his own age.

Helping With Homework

Kids need your help with their homework. Teachers don't expect you to ignore your child if she asks for help. But you shouldn't *do* your child's homework. The whole purpose of going to school is to learn stuff. And homework supports that purpose if the child does it herself.

So there's a fine line to walk with homework. It makes sense to provide a place to do the work, maybe in the kitchen where your help is nearby or in a quiet room. It makes sense to have the tools available, like paper, pencils, a calculator, a dictionary and maybe a computer. You can help your child make a plan for getting it done. And you can assist if you're asked with figuring out directions or thinking through a problem, helping your child memorize something or listening to a speech.

The purpose of school is not to get good grades, despite evidence that supports such a view. At least the grades a child earns should be just that (*earned*) and not bought or borrowed from someone else. It's hard for a parent to see a child struggle, but the solution is not to do the child's work. The solution is to support her learning so she is more successful on her own.

So when you help with homework, notice how your child's thinking is stuck. Can you provide her with background information that will clear up the present confusion? Can you teach a skill that she needs to be successful? Can you move your child toward a breakthrough moment where troublesome schoolwork suddenly makes sense?

Use the resources around you to help your child. Most schools these days have homework hotlines, and some public libraries offer free homework assistance. Help your child get on the right track without taking away from her the learning experience.

Not The End Of The World

Children who don't complete high school or who don't go on to college aren't necessarily doomed to the School of Hard Knocks. Hard work, pursuit of a passion, good social skills and a few lucky breaks can take a kid a long way.

Successful High School Drop-Outs
Wendy's franchise founder Dave Thomas
Actor Johnny Depp
Singer Christina Aguilera
Musician Tom Petty
ABC News anchor Peter Jennings
Wright Brother Orville Wright
Virgin Atlantic Airways founder Richard Branson
Entertainment empire builder Walt Disney
Beatle Ringo Starr
Charismatic royal Princess Diana
Theory of Relativity creator Albert Einstein

Successful College Drop-Outs
Actor Ben Affleck
Newsweek reporter Eleanor Clift
Computer maker Michael Dell
Senator Barry Goldwater
Microsoft founder and philanthropist Bill Gates
(This list could go on and on. In fact, only about half the people who start college finish with a degree.)

On dropping out of Harvard after only two years:

I realized the error of my ways and decided I could make do with a high school diploma.
—Microsoft founder Bill Gates

Why Kids Drop Out

In America's big cities, the high school dropout rate is as high as 50%. Despite the fact that education is accepted as the first step toward earning a decent wage, half of the kids who start high school as ninth graders don't finish all the way to the end of their senior year. Why not?

Here are the main reasons why kids drop out:

- They are older than other kids in their grade, either because they started late, were held back a year or two, or failed courses they had to repeat.

- They don't have enough credits to graduate even though they've been enrolled in high school for four years. They failed courses, took the wrong courses, or skipped too many classes.

- They don't see the value of finishing because the best jobs in their neighborhoods are minimum-wage jobs they could get even without a high school diploma.

- They've been kicked out of their homes or their families are homeless. Without a permanent place to live, only the most determined kids can finish school.

- They don't fit in. Socially, intellectually, or creatively they just don't "get" high school and are happier out of it.

Some of these problems are within your control. Even when there are problems outside your control, it's worth helping your kid stick with high school and graduate. But notice this: kids who drop out of school are not stupid. Instead, most dropouts are capable, even exceptional kids who needed more support than they got.

Do what you can to support your kids.

Finding The Money

A high school senior I know was offered a full athletic scholarship to an elite college. His parents saw this as just the ticket. The young man did not. He didn't want to attend that school, no matter how good the deal.

A kid who is mature enough to go to college is mature enough to make the decision of where to enroll. It's not about money. It's about fit. His parents wisely backed off.

Nonetheless, it's hard not to think of the money. With the cost of college spiraling higher more quickly than just about any other segment of the economy, parents are justifiably worried about paying tuition.

But remember this:
- Where a child attends college is not so important as being happy and successful once she's there.
- Colleges are businesses (even the tax-supported ones). If your child wants to attend a particular school, that school wants to enroll her.
- Never squelch a favorite choice of college just because the sticker price is ridiculously high. Apply and get admitted. Let the school make its best deal.
- Negotiate just as you'd negotiate any other big-ticket item. Be prepared to walk away and attend another school.

Again, the prestige of the college a kid attends is not so important as being happy and successful once he's there. A full-ride scholarship is terrific, but not if it's at the wrong school.

Off To College

When my older son told me he wanted to major in fine art my first impulse was to change his mind. I suggested he at least earn a second major in something more practical. But he ignored my advice, graduated in art and became a highly sought-after designer and artist.

Of course, it helps that in the time it took him to complete his degree, the world became much more focused on visual media. How things look is much more important these days than it used to be. Just look at book covers from the 1970's and the cover of this book, for example. But that just points out that it's hard to predict the value of any college major. Things change, and much of the time, kids are better at seeing the future than their parents are.

So the best advice you can give your child is "major in what you like." Passion and enthusiasm are excellent predictors of career success.

College is expensive and parents naturally want to see a return on their investment. But the return is not so much in a job title (like "my daughter the lawyer" or "my son the physicist") but in an ability to think clearly, defend an argument, write persuasively, and solve problems. A college-educated person these days has more tools than someone who didn't go to college, regardless of what her college major was or what her first job is after graduation.

The choice of a college and of a major might be your child's first really big decisions. Let her make them herself. Let her change her mind if she feels like it. This is the beginning of her adulthood and the start of your role as an observer, not an active player, in her life. It's a time when you help her make her own decisions, not by giving advice, but by asking questions that help her to think things through on her own.

.

Becoming A Reader
The key step in school success

It Starts Before You Know It

We sometimes say that a baby is learning to talk when she first starts to make language-like sounds late in the first year. We forget that babies start learning language even before birth while they listen in to conversations from inside the womb. By the time toddlers actually can talk, they have been working on this all-important skill for a long time.

In the same way, learning to read doesn't start at age five or six. Kids pick up on elements of reading from infancy onward. Finally being able to read is the culmination of a lot of small developmental steps.

So waiting until kindergarten to work on reading skills is not a good idea. But what those "reading skills" are is not what you might expect. No parent needs to teach a child to read, if by teaching you mean making a child recite what is printed on a page. But every parent can do simple, everyday things that will prepare a child for reading instruction in school. Every parent can help a child be "ready to read."

The first and most important thing you can do is give your child confidence to try hard things. We do this when babies are learning to walk. We don't criticize a child who falls down but we cheer when he picks himself back up and wobbles ahead. We don't expect perfection too soon. The same is true for reading. While reading might seem to come naturally to some people, reading is still not something that just happens. We have to learn how to read. We have to be taught.

Are You A Reader?

There's a lot of things to read in the world. How many of these have you read in the past month or two?

- ☐ A novel (spy novel, romance novel, mystery, etc.)
- ☐ Directions on how to do something
- ☐ Material on the Internet
- ☐ A children's book
- ☐ A screen play
- ☐ A recipe
- ☐ A newspaper
- ☐ A magazine
- ☐ A short story
- ☐ A catalogue
- ☐ Letters
- ☐ Email
- ☐ A non-fiction book
- ☐ Comics
- ☐ A graphic novel
- ☐ An interview
- ☐ Poetry
- ☐ A television schedule
- ☐ A movie review

Some people believe that "a reader" is someone they're not and someone they don't want to be. They're pretty comfortable with this choice. But it's hard for a child to value something that his parent rejects.

Having a small child is an opportunity for you to rediscover your inner reader. Try to take advantage of that chance. Find something to read.

Why Is Reading So Important?

Reading is certainly the cornerstone of school success. The child who struggles to read well by the fourth grade will be unable to learn all the material presented in the upper grades and high school. The child who doesn't read also doesn't write and can't even take notes on class lectures. The non-reader is clearly at a huge disadvantage in school. In fact, our schools really are not equipped to deal with a child who doesn't read.

But school success isn't the only reason that reading is important. The written word is the key to civilization. Because human beings can write, they can keep track of events and remember and learn from past experience. Because humans can write, they can ponder their own feelings and the meaning of their own existence. Certainly these things can happen without writing—we can simply tell each other things and pass stories from generation to generation—but the written word forms a more stable record.

Reading is important because it puts a whole lot of information at our disposal. We don't need to keep everything mankind has ever known in our own memories. To tap the wisdom of the past and the ideas and feelings of others, we need to be able to read about them.

Spoken language is short-lived. When we stop talking, it's gone. Written language is language preserved. We can come back to it again and again. You want your child to be able to do that. It's worth the trouble to help your child become a reader.

Books And Vocabulary

Books are a great source of new words since authors often pick just the right word for a situation, not the most common word. So reading with your child and talking about the words you run into is a great way to expand your kid's reading and thinking skills.

A young man who is heavily into *Calvin and Hobbes* books recently mentioned reading the word "salubrious" in a cartoon. That sent both of us to the dictionary to find out what it meant. We found ways to use it the rest of the day. (It means "healthful.")

I'm reading the classic book *Charlotte's Web* with a grandchild these days. Here are some words we've noticed and enjoyed from that book:

bloodthirsty	manure
carriage	miracle
crisis	radiant
glory	runt
glutton	salutations
gullible	slops
humble	snout
injustice	triumph
languish	trough
magnum opus	versatile

These aren't words my grandchild can read. Some of them I can barely read myself. But these are words that have enriched the story for us and made us smarter as we've read them.

Conversation Is The Key

For children to read words, they have to *know* words. The bigger a kid's vocabulary, the easier it will be for him to learn to read. And it's not just words but phrases and the way people talk. Building a vocabulary isn't accomplished by memorizing the dictionary. It's not just learning words in isolation. Building a vocabulary is learning to put words together in sentences and learning what words go together.

To have a store of words and phrases, children need to hear words and phrases. They need conversation. So an important part of helping a child become a reader is talking with him. Tell him things, yes, but also ask *him* to tell *you* things. Explain things and ask him to think of explanations too. Research indicates that the more adults talk with children, the bigger the children's vocabularies and the more successful they are in school.

Notice that talking *with* your child is not the same as talking *to* your child. The same research that indicates "the more talking the more school success" also reports that kids who are given a lot of commands and who are expected to listen to adults but are not listened to themselves have *smaller vocabularies* than kids who have more opportunities for real conversation. Children need to hear a wide range of language, and they have to *use* a wide range of language. Talk with your children a lot and make sure they talk with you too.

The need for children to use language as well as hear language points out one reason why watching television is not strongly associated with learning to read. No matter how "educational" the program, listening to television is no substitute for real conversation with caring and interested adults. So while kids certainly can watch TV, don't think that watching television gets you off the hook for hanging out with your children. It doesn't. Talk with your kids.

Story Ideas

Do you remember favorite stories you were told when you were a kid? List some here.

What stories from your family history would make good tales to tell? Write those here.

The Power Of Story

Having a rich vocabulary is an advantage to the young reader. But vocabulary alone is not enough, because what we read is not just words. We read stories.

We're so used to how stories unfold (and the word "story" here can mean anything from fairy stories to news stories) that we forget that we adults have actually learned what a story is like. A story has a beginning, a middle and an end. The sentences in a story all describe what the story is about and not something else. A story has a point or a conclusion that is satisfying or makes sense.

Children who are ready to read understand what stories are. They've developed expectations that help them to follow a story as they read and to anticipate what might happen next. They are open to surprise and suspense because they know that those are common story elements. And how do they know all this? They know because they've heard stories.

So tell stories to your child. Tell stories about your day together ("We went to Grandma's and guess who was there? Uncle Bob!"). Tell stories about what you and your child are going to do ("First, we're going to buy you some shoes. Then we will go to the park and swing on the swings"). Tell stories about the day your child was born or the day you adopted your cat or the day you moved to this apartment.

And help your child to tell stories to you. Ask what he's doing and listen to his answer. Ask what he had for lunch at child care or who he played with on the playground. If your child can describe things to you, he is well on his way to being a reader. He understands what a story does.

Great Books For Younger Kids

My favorite picture books

Caps for Sale by Esphyr Slobodkina
Home for a Bunny by Margaret Wise Brown
Little Bear by Else Holmelund Minarek
Millions of Cats by Wanda Gag
The Mitten by Alvin Tresselt
Where the Wild Things Are by Maurice Sendak

What are *your* favorite picture books?

Chapter books for younger listeners

Charlotte's Web by E. B. White
James and the Giant Peach by Roald Dahl
My Father's Dragon by Ruth Stiles Gannett
The Hobbit by J. R. R. Tolkien
The Wonderful Wizard of Oz by Frank L. Baum

What are your favorite chapter books for young kids?

Great sources for more book ideas

Book Crush: For Kids and Teens by Nancy Perl
The Read-Aloud Handbook by Jim Trelease

How To Read To A Child

One of the great things about *telling* a story to a child is that you can adjust the story as you go along. You can make the story fit the child right now and can change the story again as she grows older and is more ready for the whole version. You can do this with a book too.

The key to reading to your child is to make the reading more of a conversation than a recitation. Take your cue from the child and talk about what on the page interests her. Don't feel you have to read the words verbatim. It's okay to use words that fit your child's understanding. And just because you start a book doesn't mean you have to read it all or read it all in order. Your allegiance is to your child, not to the author of the book.

Especially with a very small child, sit together and admire the pictures first. Go through the book slowly, reading what seems good to read and just talking about the rest. The next time you read this book, you might read more and talk less or you may find other things to discuss.

When you read to an older child, it's okay to stop and talk about what's happening in the story. Speculate together about what might happen next or how the main character is feeling. If there's an interesting word look at how it's written and pronounced (my five-year-old grandson was delighted by the word "nincompoop" in Roald Dahl's *James and the Giant Peach*).

Whether you're reading to a baby or to an older kid, be sure to read with feeling. Nothing is more dull than listening to someone read in a monotone, as if the words meant nothing. Enjoy yourself. Read books you really like so enjoying yourself is easier.

Read Aloud To Big Kids Too

You can keep your older child interested in reading by reading together books you both enjoy. Here are some ideas.

The Borrowers by Mary Norton
Treasure Island by Robert Louis Stevenson
Frankenstein by Mary Shelley
The Lord of the Rings by J. R. R. Tolkien
To Kill a Mockingbird by Harper Lee
Tom Sawyer by Mark Twain
The Black Cauldron by Lloyd Alexander
The *Harry Potter* books by J. K. Rowling
Redwall by Brian Jacques
Little Women by Louisa May Alcott
The Willoughbys by Lois Lowry
Alice in Wonderland by Lewis Carroll
The Lion, the Witch and the Wardrobe by C. S. Lewis
The Hitchhiker's Guide to the Galaxy by Douglas Adams
Mysteries of *Sherlock Holmes* by Arthur Conan Doyle

What other good books do these remind you of?

Reading And The Older Child

As kids grow up they sort themselves into those who read all the time and those who read only when they have to. Obviously the kids who read more read better than the kids who read less. How can you help your reluctant reader to read more?

Get the right books into your kid's hands.

The "right books" might be books of cartoons or comic strips. They might be comic books. They might be books of world records, bizarre events, and "believe it or not" facts. Try books about whatever your kid is interested in, whether it's ghosts, NASCAR, football, video game play, or space aliens. Find books that aren't really books, but are websites, magazines, or movie scripts.

Many kids who don't read much enjoy writing instead. Your child might like creating a comic strip or television episode or writing fan letters.

Another way to help your child enjoy stories is to find books-on-tape (on CD or as downloads). The entire book is read by professional readers or even by the author himself.

Read aloud to your child for as long as she'll let you, into her teens if you can. By sharing good books that you both like, with you reading everything or the two of you taking turns, you'll not only share the literary experience but share a great time with each other. Just be sure to let this experience be enjoyable and not a test of her ability to read well.

How do you find books your older child will like? Talk to your local bookstore clerk. He will know what kids like yours are reading.

More Than One Way To Shine
Helping your child find his strengths

Multiple Paths To Success

One of the great things about having kids is you get to experience things (good things) that you didn't get to experience in your own childhood. You get to see the world through your child's eyes. And this is an opportunity that shouldn't be missed.

So it's important to stay open to whatever your child chooses for her hobbies, school courses, college major and career goals. Not every happy, successful adult is a prestigious physician or attorney. In fact, neither satisfaction in life nor financial success are related to being the top student in high school. Most millionaires in America run Mom-and-Pop businesses like gas stations and mini-marts. A lot of millionaires were high school dropouts.

So, while of course you want your kid to stay in school, you also want him to follow his own path to success. Try not to steer him too forcefully into the way you'd like him to go. Your dreams may not be his dreams.

At the same time, remember that people these days have serial careers. Most adults do not work in fields directly related to their college majors. Most adults wind up in careers that no one could've predicted from what they did for their first jobs.

Satisfaction and success in life are not the destination. They are instead pleasures to be had along the way.

What's Your Intelligence Profile?

Howard Gardner believes everyone has a different intelligence profile across nine talent areas. What is your own intelligence profile? What do you think matches your child's profile and the profile of your child's other parent?

Language, including vocabulary, reading, and writing
I see this in myself ☐   *my child* ☐   *my child's other parent* ☐

Mathematics and logic
I see this in myself ☐   *my child* ☐   *my child's other parent* ☐

Spatial abilities, like art, architecture, and arrangement
I see this in myself ☐   *my child* ☐   *my child's other parent* ☐

Music
I see this in myself ☐   *my child* ☐   *my child's other parent* ☐

Physical coordination, speed and strength
I see this in myself ☐   *my child* ☐   *my child's other parent* ☐

Interpersonal skill in negotiating and persuading
I see this in myself ☐   *my child* ☐   *my child's other parent* ☐

Intrapersonal skill in self-understanding and insight
I see this in myself ☐   *my child* ☐   *my child's other parent* ☐

Affinity for nature, including plants and animals
I see this in myself ☐   *my child* ☐   *my child's other parent* ☐

Spiritual and metaphysical understanding, including morality and supernatural ideas
I see this in myself ☐   *my child* ☐   *my child's other parent* ☐

What Your Kid Does Naturally

Neuroscientist and educational philosopher Howard Gardner believes that our talents and inclinations are hard-wired into our brains. His Multiple Intelligences theory suggests that people are at their best when they work to their strengths. Gardner even advocates testing young children to see what their brain-based abilities are and then focusing their educations toward those.

Much of the American educational system is focused on only a couple of brain-based abilities: language arts and math. Kids who have natural talent in these areas excel in school. Kids whose natural talents lie in other areas, like art, physical coordination, or music, for example, might have more trouble in school or might feel that school isn't right for them.

Obviously, every child needs to learn to read, write and do math. It's hard to function without these skills. But clearly not every school child is going to be an A student. This doesn't mean the C students are hopelessly mediocre. It just means that school's focus doesn't match the C student's talents.

One of your jobs as a parent, then, is to figure out what your kid's talents and natural inclinations are. You can then provide extra-curricular experiences to develop those talents. Extra-curricular experiences can be classes or organized activities, but also they can be just your interest and support.

If Gardner is right (and I think he is) then natural inclinations can be observed early in a child's life. Because they are often inherited, your own abilities, including the ones you've hidden from the world, may be abilities your child has too. So take a long look at your child. Where do his natural talents lie?

Did You Have A "That's It!" Moment?

Have you had an experience where you suddenly knew what you wanted to do with your life or wanted to be good at? If you did, write about it here.

Do you remember wishing to do something that you never got around to doing or that you finally did get to do? Write about those things here.

Is there something you intend to do just as soon as you can? What will you do when you retire or as soon as you make enough money? Write about that here.

If your child had a "That's It!" moment, what was it or what would it be?

Life-Changing Experiences

Howard Gardner, the creator of Multiple Intelligences theory, tells the story of musician Yehudi Menuhin who heard a violin for the first time at age three. Menuhin felt an immediate connection and at that moment decided that he would play the violin.

Far-fetched? Far from it. Many of us can look back and think of a moment when we "first knew" we had a particular talent or interest. Usually these moments were unplanned. Just as Menuhin's parents may have taken him to the symphony on a whim, not thinking they were launching a distinguished career, so it often happens that we are surprised by what strikes a chord in us and in our kids.

So what this means for us parents is two things.

First, provide your child with a variety of experiences, including (maybe "especially including") experiences of really high-quality. It's hard to be inspired to learn the violin at a middle-school concert. Include experiences that might seem at first to be a stretch or off the beaten path. It's hard to predict what might really inspire your kid.

Second, pick up on hints and cues that your child might provide. Notice if your kid seems to have a talent for working with his hands or enjoys acting out stories or something. Try to support these inclinations.

But be careful that you don't push an agenda of your own or take over your child's interests. Imagine that you announced you're training for a 5-K race and someone said, "Oh, that's great. I know an expert on that and a great place to get shoes, and the best place to train" and so on and so on. That's nice, but it sort of crushes your own interest. So don't take over your kid's life. Just give him a glimpse of what's out there and what's possible.

Endless Possibilities

What classes and programs could inspire your child and tap into his hidden talents? Which of these did you try as a child?

My child		I tried this
_____	Team sports	_____
_____	Individual sports	_____
_____	Competitive games, like chess	_____
_____	Martial arts	_____
_____	Language classes	_____
_____	Art and crafts	_____
_____	Dance	_____
_____	Acting or modeling	_____
_____	Movie making	_____
_____	Computer programming	_____
_____	Video game development	_____
_____	Running a junior business	_____
_____	Caring for a pet or livestock	_____
_____	Cooking	_____
_____	Sewing, quilting, knitting	_____
_____	Singing, choir	_____
_____	Classical music or band	_____
_____	Rock music or jazz	_____
_____	Church school, volunteering	_____
_____	Scouts, Camp Fire, etc	_____
_____	Writing, having a pen pal	_____
_____	Gardening	_____
_____	Rocket building, model making	_____
_____	Inventing, collecting	_____
_____	Specialty camps or tutoring	_____

How Scheduled Is Over-Scheduled?

One way to provide inspiring experiences that tap into your child's latent talents is to sign her up for classes and coaching. The possibilities are endless.

And that's the problem. You can't choose them all, but some parents seem to want to.

Remember that childhood and even the teen years are times to sample things and discover what your kid likes and is good at. It's not the time to launch her career. Granted there are children who become celebrities for one reason or another before they're old enough to vote. But most kids are on a more developmentally appropriate track.

So keep some perspective. Let your child participate in extra-curricular activities at school, do things in the community, and take classes outside school. But no child should have so many activities that he has no time for friendships or for just hanging out. One or maybe two after-school programs a week are plenty for most kids.

But what if your child wants to experience more than one or two extra things? What then?

Keep in mind that not every activity needs to become a life-time commitment. A child can take lessons for six weeks and then take a completely different set of lessons after that. Just because your kid signed up for tennis this season doesn't mean he has to continue training in the off-season. If the interest is there, fine. If it's not, don't push it.

Discouraging Facts About Teen Work

1. Most teen workers are supervised by other teens. They're not being mentored by role-model adults.

2. Many teen jobs encourage slacker behavior instead of good work habits. Ways to look busy without doing anything, how to take long breaks and even how to sabotage an employer are part of the teen job scene.

3. Many teen jobs are dangerous. Jobs operating machinery, construction jobs, and delivery jobs are actually prohibited for teens but are among the jobs teens take.

4. Teens who work tend to get less sleep than other kids and do less well in school.

5. Teens who work in high school tend to have lower incomes as adults than other kids.

6. Most income earned by teens is spent on consumer goods and entertainment. Only a very small percentage of teen income nationally is saved for college.

7. To make enough after-tax income to buy the things teens crave requires more minimum-wage hours than can be fit into the end of a school day.

Should Your Teen Get A Job?

For some families, this question is a no-brainer. "Yes, my kid should get a job because our family has to have the extra income." In the perilous economy of the past several years, many hard-working parents rely on their equally hard-working teens to make ends meet. Kids who can shoulder this sort of responsibility without resentment deserve a lot of credit.

But for many families, teen income is spent only on teen desires. And for these families, taking a job to support teens' purchasing power can be an issue. On the one hand, parents want to be able to say, "If you want that, you'll have to pay for it yourself." On the other hand, parents know that to do a good job in school and be prepared for a good-paying job in the future, teens need to devote only the minimum time now to minimum-wage jobs.

What's the answer?

The answer is clearer if your family has managed to avoid buying in to the cult of consumerism. If your children grew up placing value in people and experiences instead of in things, they will have fewer desires that need a job to fund.

The answer is clearer if your child can find a job that is more an apprenticeship than just a job. A position in a computer firm, law office, special education unit, or design company may add to your kid's education instead of interfering with it.

Real-life experience can be valuable. But most teen jobs provide experience in things that are not worth the cost in lost sleep, poor grades, and real danger. Think over the need for teen work carefully and weigh all the options.

Guilt Trips

Any time we tell children, "If you loved me, you'd do what I want," we interfere with their independence. Any time we even *imply* that message or make children *think* that message, we hold them hostage to our will.

And that, you'll recall, is not what you want to do. You want your kids to grow up, become masters of their universes, and leave home for lovely lives of their own.

It's easy to inflict guilt. When my boys wanted to spend their allowance, my stock answer used to be, "If that's what you really want." I didn't intend to question their ability to make decisions (at least I don't think I did). But that was the effect. It seemed to my kids that I wanted them to guess what I was thinking about how to spend their money, not figure it out on their own. One of my boys finally told me to cut it out and I came to my senses.

How much did guilt figure into your relationship with your parents? Is guilt still a tool used against you, even though you're an adult? Do you use guilt with your own kids?

A Question Of Commitment

When I bought my middle-school son an electric guitar for his birthday, he was upset. He said he "didn't want the commitment." Although this kid grew up to become a superb guitarist and although music is an important part of his life as an adult, his first thought, obviously, was "What are you trying to get me into?"

Oh, dear.

It's easy to overplay your hand when you want the best for your kids. It's easy to appear to kids like the ancient Greeks who gave their enemies a wonderful statue of a horse, only to have this "gift" open and release a horde of soldiers. Your best efforts to understand your children's talents and provide the right tool at the right time to release this potential can backfire. You can be viewed suspiciously. Is this gift a Trojan horse?

So your gifts should contain no conquering hordes. You must be prepared for your efforts to be rejected or tried and discarded. Only your kids know if what you've offered fits who they are and what they're prepared to try today. The light you're trying to fan into brightness might not be ready to shine. You can only offer. It's your kids who have to supply the commitment.

So your gift (of a guitar, of Spanish lessons, or of damp Saturdays cheering from the soccer sidelines) comes with no strings attached. No guilt trip gets laid on if the gift is later set aside.

You are committed, not to the gift, but to your child.

Disruptions And Detours
Helping children cope with change

Change Is Natural. Change Is Hard.

Everything changes. It's surprising that we can be surprised by change since it's the one thing we can always be sure of. But we are never ready.

Part of the problem is that we can stand some small changes as long as the important things stay the same. But we have no more control over the important things than we have over the piddly ones. We can stand having our kids grow up as long as they don't fall ill. We can stand losing a job as long as we don't lose the house.

But sometimes we have to withstand the unbearable. We don't have any choice. And when we're in that difficult place our kids are there with us. We not only have to deal with change ourselves but we have to help our children manage it too. How do you do that? Here's some tips:

- Tell no lies. Tell truths that will not have to be revised as your kids grow older or hear things from others.
- Be matter-of-fact. Share your feelings honestly but there's no need to increase the emotional drama.
- Don't point fingers. Identifying the person who is "at fault" doesn't help anything and causes lasting harm.
- Move forward. Today is different from yesterday, but that doesn't mean you can give up on tomorrow.

Look ahead. Your life and your children's lives take place in the future. Embrace all the experiences ahead.

Home Is Where The Heart Is

What are your childhood memories of home? Did you move away from a home you loved? Did you move to a home that turned out wonderfully?

Write about your memories of home.

Moving Away

Our family made a cross-country move the year our younger son was three. He left a best buddy who lived next door, a familiar preschool, and a backyard creek full of crayfish. He told me with all sincerity, "You've ruined my life."

If a three-year-old can feel this strongly about moving to a new home, it's easy to see how older children and teens can feel equally done-to. Clearly, my son blamed Mom and Dad for his forced removal. Moving is difficult enough for a grown-up, who at least chose to make the move or knows the reasons behind it. How hard it must be for a child who can never really understand.

But you should try to help him understand. It's never a good idea to announce a move to a new home suddenly or casually. You don't want your child to feel like just a piece of furniture that can be packed up and hauled off without explanation. The more time your child has before the move, the more included he will feel in the process. You can include him in finding out about the new town or neighborhood and maybe even take him along on house-hunting or apartment-hunting trips. Older children can research their new schools online and use maps to figure out the closest playground or sports center in your new location.

Help your child before the move to assemble memories of the old place. She can take digital photos of her favorite people and her old house. The family can make a sort of farewell tour of well-loved haunts before finally packing up and moving away.

Moving is a leave-taking but it's also an arrival. Help your child see the silver lining and new opportunities hidden in the move.

The Best Revenge

You know that "living well is the best revenge" and revenge is extra sweet when living well helps your kids too.

So model the very best behavior toward your ex. Doing so will set an example for your children and will take the steam out of your ex's subterfuges. Let things bounce off you. Return anger with a smile.

If there are problems that have to be addressed, bring those up—politely, like a reasonable adult—when your children are not around. Really big problems are your attorney's territory. Let her handle them.

Your ex doesn't care about your feelings. If your feelings mattered, you two wouldn't be living apart. So acting hurt and angry will get you nowhere. On the other hand, acting like you are too self-confident and mature to let your ex's petty maneuvers bother you will make those maneuvers look immature and desperate.

Sweet.

Separation And Divorce

For children, divorce can feel worse than the death of a parent. A death isn't planned but separation and divorce are *created intentionally*. Children know that intention matters.

Children wonder how their parents could have fallen out of love. But they wonder too whether they themselves were the cause. Many children in divorce feel guilty and anxious. "If you no longer love each other," kids think, "will you someday no longer love me?"

Children's feelings get forgotten while parents hash things out. Children feel pulled apart. The child in the middle of custody negotiations feels like an object, not a person. It comes as no surprise that children in divorce often act out. Instead of yelling at each other, Mom and Dad can yell at the child. For many children, this is preferable.

So what can you do if separation and divorce are unavoidable? A few things make a big difference.

- Dial down the anger and aggression. Be nice to each other no matter how hard it is.

- Put your children's needs and interests first in working toward a legal resolution. What is best for the kids will be better for each of the parents too.

- Remain cordial toward your ex. Both of you will continue to share your children's lives for their entire lives. Make the future tolerable for all.

- Remember that things cannot take the place of the relationships that were damaged. Trying to replace a parent with toys feels false even to children.

Divorce can trigger a cascade of changes that are unsettling for kids. Even though the parents are hurting too, they've got to put the children first.

Gains And Losses

If your family has added a new family member or is planning to, take some time to consider how this will affect your child. What will the child see as a positive outcome of this change? What will the child see as a negative outcome?

Gains from the child's point of view

Losses from the child's point of view

What can you do to develop the gains and dampen the losses?

New Family Members

The addition of new people to love should be a happy thing. And it usually is for adults in the family. Mom and Dad are delighted with a new baby or newly adopted child. A remarried parent is thrilled to welcome a new spouse and the new spouse's children. Even moving Grandma into the spare bedroom is a good thing for adults who would worry about her otherwise.

But for the children in the family, these new people create serious disruptions of the social order. Kids wonder whether they have to obey the new spouse. They worry they might have to share their rooms or their toys with the new spouse's children. They resent the attention given to the new family member, even a new baby. Kids know that attention is a zero-sum game: the more that's given to someone else, the less there is for them. And what about Grandma? She seems to be living in 1975.

It's not hard to see why adding new family members can be troublesome, no matter who is added or why.

This doesn't mean families have to stay the same. But it does mean that you can't expect changes in family membership to be welcomed by one and all. There will be a period of adjustment and there will be rough spots that need to be smoothed out.

Anticipate issues and resolve them ahead of time as much as you can. Then deal with issues as they come up. Don't sweep them under the rug or deny they exist.

Kids have problems with adding new people, even if they love the new people dearly. Ask your child, "How's this working out for you?" and really listen to what is said. Just knowing you care will make the transition easier.

A New Reality

Change alters the landscape. Not only is the present moment shattered, but the future is foreclosed. Your family is suddenly transported to new territory. How do you figure out the lay of the land? Where do you go from here?

Where you can't go is back to where you were. Many people spin their wheels in the face of change, trying to get back to "normal." But normal has shifted. It's not possible to go back there again.

What's the "new normal" for you and your children, now that a big change has happened? How will you all find happiness and satisfaction even in this new reality? You can do it if you set your mind to it. Start that here.

Illness And Injury

"Into each life some rain must fall," my dad used to say, quoting Longfellow's poem. Almost every family experiences a serious illness or injury of one of its members sometime during the children's lives.

But we're always surprised. Illness and injury (and other sudden losses, like a house fire) catch us unprepared. Parents are absorbed immediately in fixing the problem. In the space of a heartbeat or phone call, the world shifts and kids are not the center of attention any more.

This is as it should be. Catastrophes demand action and parents have to focus on that. But at the same time, children's worries have to be addressed. As much as possible, children need to know what is going on. They need to know, even though Mom and Dad are distracted, that the children's needs are still important. And they have to know that they are safe. Mom and Dad are on the case. Things will be all right.

A physical injury is often easier for children to understand than an illness. A mental illness is hardest for children to grasp. But all injuries and illnesses are likely to be met by anger, as the child rebels against the affected person's lack of responsiveness. The child may develop sympathetic symptoms herself. Children may act out at school or be withdrawn and depressed. Children may be mean to their siblings and even to the affected person.

Help is available and stressed parents should take advantage of it. Your child's school and the hospital both have counseling services. Ask about this. Certainly let your child's teacher know what's going on. And take time to talk with your child and let him share his anger and sadness. A crisis is a time to hold tightly together.

Your Views On An Afterlife

Figure out what you will tell your child when death raises questions. What do you believe?

Do you believe that what is essential in a person lives on after death in some way?
- If so, how do you envision this "living on"?
- If so, does this apply to all people?
- If so, does this apply to pets and other animals?

Does what you believe affect your thoughts about causing the death of another being, including bugs and pests?

What can you tell a child about the fate of the body itself after death?
- Can you describe this in relation to an animal, including a pet?
- Can you describe this in relation to a human being?

How can you help your child remember the deceased being fondly?
- What stories can be told and retold?
- What artifacts can be treasured, including pictures?
- What things can be let go, including unpleasant memories?

What do you believe about rituals like funerals and memorial services?
- Would you conduct something like this after the death of an animal that was not a pet?
- Would you conduct something like this after the death of a pet?
- Would you include your child in something like this after the death of a human being?

Death

Where death is concerned, most of us are still like children. We don't want to talk about it. We don't understand it. We are afraid and fascinated at the same time. Being a parent provides us with an opportunity to come to grips with death so we can point our children in the right direction.

Take advantage of the small deaths that bump into your child's life. Talk about the dead bird on the sidewalk. Consider the goldfish that goes belly-up. What is it that's missing in a dead thing that was present when it was alive? What does being dead mean?

For some parents, these questions have a religious or spiritual answer. Figure out what you believe and figure out if you and the child's other parent share the same views. Even if you don't believe in an afterlife, realize that your child will encounter this idea from other kids. Do some thinking on the topic so you are sure of what you want to say when your child asks.

The death of a beloved pet or a human being is much more powerful than the demise of a goldfish. You will be sad too. You, like your child, will be puzzled and upset by death. There is no need to pretend to have all the answers or to hide your grief. Death is a great leveler. Children and adults are equally affected and equally mystified. Be honest with your child and own your feelings.

Find a child-size memorial to enact or create. Assure your child that he is still safe. Help your child understand that he's not going to die immediately too. Get professional help for him if he seems to need it. Get professional help for yourself if you need it.

It's okay not to have all the answers.

Put On Your Own Mask First

You're familiar with the airline instructions "in case of a sudden decrease in cabin pressure." Oxygen masks, you're told, will drop from the overhead compartment and you should put one on over your nose and mouth. If you're traveling with children, you should put on your own mask first, then help your kids.

Good advice and not just for air travel.

When your family is hit by a crisis and then another crisis follows that and another and another, it's important to take care of yourself first. Get help from a reliable professional or get some support from a friend or relative. You can't help your kids weather the storm if you yourself are falling apart.

Free guidance is available. Contact your child's school or your doctor. Call a crisis hotline. Make an appointment with your area's human services department. No one knows you need help until you tell him. Don't be too proud or embarrassed or busy putting out fires to seek the help you need.

By helping yourself, you will help your kids. They are relying on you to be strong, especially in difficult times.

Do Things Come In Threes?

My mother used to think bad things happen in triplicate. After two bad events (airline crashes were her specialty) she would wait for the third with anxious anticipation. Often changes in your children's lives come in bunches too, like dominoes falling in a line.

- A divorce might lead to moving to a new home.
- A new baby might require the family to move to a new home or deal with an illness or disability.
- Remarriage of one parent or the other might mean new family members, and maybe a new home as well.
- Serious illness or injury might lead to a death.
- Illness, divorce and death all mean someone whom children counted on is missing from their daily lives.

One change often follows another. Children can feel the world is shifting under their feet. It shouldn't be a surprise that many kids react badly to change.

Resilient children are kids who trust that grown-ups are in charge. They know that though it seems their world is falling apart, the center of their lives is steady. Mom and Dad are still running the ship. Children are allowed to be children. Things will be all right.

Your task in times of turmoil is to remember that change is the natural state of the world. Change doesn't come in threes; it comes continually. Your kids will learn to accept the ups and downs of life by watching you.

Making It All Better
What to do if you've screwed up

To Err Is Human

When my older son was a baby, I clonked him on the head. It was an accident, of course. I had the baby in my arms, talking to a plumber who had come to fix the pipes. I turned to talk about something behind me, and bonked the baby's head against the doorframe. Ouch!

I've thought of this moment often in the thirty years since. The boy turned out fine, but what if he hadn't? What if I'd made a terrible mistake?

It happens. Big, awful, careless mistakes that are instant disasters. Small, repeated, ignorant mistakes that add up to a childhood of misery. We're sorry. We acted badly. We didn't mean it at all. Or maybe we did, but for just that one moment. We see now that we've screwed up. Big time.

Or maybe our mistake was not something we did but something we should've done and didn't. Did we know at the time we were neglecting a responsibility? Or is it only now, with 20-20 hindsight, that we can see we should've acted or acted sooner?

Whether they're things we do wrong or things we don't do right, mistakes are part of parenting. The only people who never make a mistake in raising children are the people who never had any kids. It's not possible to be a parent and make no mistakes. So what do you do when you've screwed up?

Stand By Me

There may come a time when your kid will do something regrettable. What do you do then? Do you join with the legal system or school system or whatever system she has offended by rejecting her? Or do you help her endure this stressful time and come out on the other side?

Did you ever put your parents in such a position as a teen or young adult? If so, did your parents provide moral support or did they add to your punishment? Whatever your parents' reaction, did it help you? Do you feel you grew more mature as a result of your parents' response?

A kid's misbehavior is a common source of guilt and regret for parents. We think, "If only I'd seen the warning signs" and "I should've taken action earlier." Consider how you will deal with your feelings. And consider:

What does my child need right now?

How can I provide that?

What will my child need in the future?

You will be disappointed by whatever has happened. You might feel embarrassed and betrayed. These are strong feelings. But pause a long time before writing off your child. He will still need you. Don't compound the regret you feel now by reacting in a way that will cause you to feel regretful even more.

Accepting The Present As It Is

The arrow of time goes only in one direction, as near as we can tell. No amount of regret will erase what's already happened. There are no do-overs.

So if you've made mistakes as a parent or if unhappy things have happened, come to terms with them. Accept the reality of how things are and figure out where to go from here.

What does your child need right now?

How can you provide that?

What will your child need in the future?

This is no time for guilt-trips. Guilt is self-indulgent. Instead, take action. Turn your regret into commitment.

My family moved when my older son was very small from a dynamic city with thriving cultural and educational opportunities to another city that had very little. I remember my first trip to the public library in the new city and wondering how I was even going to find books to read to my boy. I immediately regretted the move and wished I could move back.

This was not the time for whining, though. Since the new town had no museums, we made the world our museum. We explored nearby creeks, bought crab nets and tanks for temporary animal guests and learned a lot about what the new area had to offer. When we moved again to a bigger, more attractive town a few years later, we took with us great memories and a first-hand knowledge of Nature that more than made up for other things we'd missed.

Don't waste time. Do what you can with what you've got.

Identify Your Priorities

Number these priorities in order of their importance to you. Use 1 for the most important and 7 for the least important. Use each number only once.

____ What my boss or clients need or expect
____ What my parents need or expect
____ What my children need or expect
____ What I need or expect
____ What the neighbors need or expect
____ What my spouse or ex needs or expects
____ What my pets need or expect

Now think of your day yesterday. Number these same priorities in order of how much attention each got from you. Use 1 for the item that got the most attention and 7 for the item that got the least attention, using each number only once.

____ What my boss or clients need or expect
____ What my parents need or expect
____ What my children need or expect
____ What I need or expect
____ What the neighbors need or expect
____ What my spouse or ex needs or expects
____ What my pets need or expect

Does how you spend your time match the importance you attach to each of them?

Revisiting What Matters

When you realize you've made a parenting mistake, you want to be sure you don't make that mistake again. The best way to do that is to remember what you believe is important.

Re-read the first chapters of this book. Are what you wrote there, about your wishes for your child, your own temperament, and the values you chose still accurate? Do those need any tweaking? Did you miss anything that you now realize is important?

Remember that your core values are your guide. But remember also that competing values bubble up when you're stressed. Figure out if you're having trouble acting on your core values when you're under stress.

Each year some parent leaves a child in a car in the summer heat. The tragic outcome is predictable after the fact. But before the fact—at the point when the parent is planning her day—what went wrong with her priorities? How did "caring for my child" fall lower in importance than "getting my errands done" or "taking care of stuff at work"?

We tend to think that personal relationships can wait. Because our children are always there, we focus on things that seem important right this minute. Those things have to be acted on now, because their moment is now. Our children have no particular moment. We take our kids for granted until we are forced to stop and look. Until we've really screwed up.

Be different. Think of your kids *now* from now on.

Starting Now...

Starting now, what changes will you make in your interactions with your children?

What important reasons are there for making these changes?

What specific actions will you take to make these changes?

1.

2.

3.

4.

When will you check back to see how well you're doing?

Every Day Is A New Opportunity

A father I know accidentally offended his nearly-grown son one day and hasn't heard from the kid since. He told his son that an asked-for loan would be the last and the son walked out. Not what the father expected or intended.

It's hard to repair an error once a person is gone. But every other error can be fixed. Today is the day to start.

Assuming your children are still speaking to you, changing how you interact with them can happen right now. You can start now to be more flexible, more values-driven, more other-directed. You can start now to listen more and talk less. You can treat your kids more like real people and less like objects. You can start today to take the long view instead of acting in the heat of the moment.

No matter what happened yesterday, you can do differently today. It's worth it. Healing can happen.

It's true that if the mistakes were great and the wounds are deep, it might take time for the new you to be believed. Your new perspective might never be entirely trusted. You can't control that.

But you will know. You will know that you've changed for the better. You will know that you've grown up and improved how you interact with your children.

Mistakes happen. But every day provides us with a clean slate. We get to try again.

Try again today.

Leaving Footsteps To Follow
Becoming a family leader

Your Legacy As A Parent

We're back at the beginning: what kind of parent do you want to be? What words of yours will echo in your adult children's heads as they raise your grandchildren? How will your parenting efforts advance the human condition, in their own small way?

We've learned that parenting is pretty complicated, and it's easy to make mistakes. Trying to be The Perfect Parent is an unrealistic goal. A goal like that signals that we just don't get it.

So we dial back our expectations. We aspire to be the most perfect parent we can be. We try to be a parent who keeps on learning, who tries every day to be worthy of the great gift that children are. A parent like that will be a model. She or he will be a leader who is willingly followed.

Every family has a box of old photographs. When you sift through yours, looking at the smiling faces from your childhood, what memories come to you? I hope they are fond memories of happy times or at least of supportive relationships. But whether your memories are pleasant or uncomfortable, you can create happy memories for your own kids. You can inspire them to be like you.

You're creating mental snapshots right now for your kids to carry forward. Make those images depict how you want to be remembered.

Who Has Scaffolded You?

We've been talking about your development as a parent. What has helped you become your "true self" in the parenting arena? Who has provided expertise without forcing you to see things just one way? Who or what has scaffolded your development?

Certainly your child has helped, so list your child first. Your child is the expert on himself and he has revealed things about himself that only he could know. Who else? From whom else have you learned about being a parent?

Be Remembered As A Scaffold

The great Russian psychologist Lev Vygotsky believed that children learn and develop through *scaffolded* interactions with people who already know. Think of what a scaffold is. It's a support structure that permits something to be built and then is taken away once that something can stand on its own. This is what you do in your best efforts as a parent.

When you are on your game as a parent, you provide your child with structure (rules, limits, methods, and strategies) that serve as the base from which your child can make progress. As your child develops his own abilities and adopts as his own the things he's learned from you, you can remove yourself (take down the scaffold) and let your child stand on his own two feet. He's ready to be an adult.

So your role as a parent is to guide and support your child but not to smother his own initiative. You give him freedom and limits.

If you've done this well, at some point the tables will turn or at least equalize. Your child will know things you don't, and *she* can scaffold *your* learning. You can ask her to explain how to create a pivot table or help you market your artwork or something. She will grow to be a lot like you, expert in many things and able to teach her expertise in a way that supports a learner.

A scaffold does not compete with the structure it supports. It's not there to force it into a particular form or to disguise it. A scaffold is temporary. Its purpose is to let another entity become its true self.

Where Is Your Refuge?

It might be a physical place, like your room or a favorite fishing spot. It might be a community, like your partner, your own parents or a support group. It might be something you can only imagine, like God or a place you remember or a place that exists only in your mind.

Who or what takes you in when you need to return to a secure base? If you don't have a secure base, what could fill that role for you?

Be Remembered As A Refuge

"Home is a place where, when you have to go there, they have to take you in," poet Robert Frost famously wrote.

Frost speaks of home as a place adults are reluctant to return to—he says "when you *have to* go there"—but also as a place where, whoever you are and whatever has happened, you will be accepted. Home and family are a refuge. A place you can always return to.

Be a refuge for your children. Be their secure base.

To be a refuge, you have to accept your children as they are, right now and into the future. They might not always do as you wish. Children can disappoint you. They may offend you. They may make choices you think are wrong-headed and dangerous. But they are still your children. Puzzling though they are, you and they are connected. Embrace that connection.

To be a refuge you have to be wise. You have life experience and a mature perspective more important and useful than maybe you realize. Even if you feel unsure of yourself much of the time, you still have wisdom, even if it's the wisdom to weigh all the alternatives before making a decision. Your children will return to you for your wise counsel if you accept your role as a refuge.

Robert Frost follows his line about home being a place where folks have to take you in with another line. He writes that home is "Something you somehow haven't to deserve." Your children need to feel accepted even if they don't feel they deserve your acceptance.

We all need that.

Practice Being Unconditional

When I was a kid, my parents gave my brothers, sister and me a weekly allowance with no strings attached. We didn't have to do chores to earn it. We didn't get paid more for doing extra chores or for getting A's on a report card. And we didn't get our allowances docked for being bad. The money was delivered unconditionally, just for being part of the family.

Money is where many families exhibit their conditional views of the world. Did you get an allowance as a child? Were there conditions attached? How would you have to change your thinking to let an allowance for your own children be *unconditional?* Write your thoughts here.

Be Remembered As Unconditional

We tend to see everything as a bargain. "If you do that, I'll let you do this." Our love and respect and acceptance are often *conditional*. We place a price on our love and offer it only if our conditions are met.

But the people who astonish us are people whose respect is *unconditional*. Those people act on the belief that we are worthy of their acceptance just the way we are. We don't have to earn it. We don't have to meet conditions. Just by being human, we are worthy of being treated humanely.

This is not easy to do. Imagine the roughest-looking person on the street corner and you'll see how hard it is to be unconditional even with your spare change. You might want to put coins in the jingling cup, but you also want to set conditions on the money: don't buy drugs or liquor. Use this to get a sandwich.

And being unconditional with love and respect is even harder with our children, for whom we have such high hopes. We act like our love is truly given only if the child gets good grades or gets into Harvard. We'll pay for a daughter's wedding only if she marries someone we like. We'll include a son in our will only if he visits us every Sunday.

Being unconditional is not the same as being indifferent. Of course we care that our kids are good people who contribute to society and who treat us nicely. The problem comes with the bargaining. Treating our love as something that can be bought by good behavior cheapens it. And expecting a child to follow our idea of what's good just to earn our love diminishes him.

Be bigger than that. Be unconditional.

Looking Forward

Looking back from your child's high school graduation to the day he was born makes you realize the impact that being a parent has had on who you are and how you think. Looking forward to the time when, though you're still a parent, your daily interactions with your child diminish, you realize that you will have a lot of free time. How will you fill it?

Some parents can't wait. They leave their kid even before their kid leaves them. But many parents feel lost and purposeless. Other parents still try to order their kids' adult lives, like a residual haunting that repeats past motions even though no one cares.

Make your plans now. How will you make the transition from parent of a child to parent of an adult? Growing up is not just for the kid, you know. It's for you too.

In It For the Long Haul

From the infant end of the telescope, being a parent seems like a long time. Eighteen years. It makes people tired just thinking about it. From the teen end of the telescope, eighteen years seems like not enough time at all. There's so much more a high school grad needs to know about life than what her parents have been able to cram into her head. Where did the time go?

Compare what you knew—or thought you knew—at your high school graduation and what you know—or think you know—now. Childhood is not the end of development; that's easy to see. There's a lot of learning and growing that happens after kids are old enough to vote. And that means that your work as a parent continues. Your job description hasn't changed. Only your supervisory authority is less.

Parenting is not just about knowledge transfer. Your work over those eighteen years is not just to impart information and get your kid a decent idea of how things work. Your contact with your adult child will not just be helping him figure out how to roast a Thanksgiving turkey or buy a house. He needs more from you than that.

No, parenting is about relationships. And the relationship you've created with your child will continue and deepen as she becomes an adult. If you've managed to develop a good relationship with your child, if you have become a leader who is willingly followed because of your support, your refuge, and your unconditional love and respect, then your life as a parent continues. It's different but the same. You're in this for the long haul.

You and your child will become more and more like peers. You will share ideas as equals or near-equals. You will go to your child for advice almost as often as he comes to you. But you've got to help it along. You can't stay stuck in your role

as a parent of young children. You have to grow up along with your kids. As we said earlier, while you're raising your children, your children are raising a parent.

The years ahead will bring new challenges to both your households. All of the disruptions and detours we talked about a bit ago will continue to interrupt your life and the lives of your children. If your kids have children of their own, you will need to adjust your parenting to this new role of being a grandparent. If your kids become so involved in their own lives that they seem to have little time for yours, then that can provide its own opportunities. Re-read the sections on control and take control of your own life. You cannot control your kids' lives.

Have you ever taught a child to ride a bicycle? Do you remember running alongside, helping him balance and keeping up his momentum? Shouting encouragement. Giving advice. At last he was able to wobble off without you, maybe forgetting to watch where he was going as he looked instead at his feet or at the space right in front of his tires. He crashed once in a while and you dusted him off and got him started again. Being a parent is like that. Being a parent is all of that right up to and including the moment your kid rides away.

That's the moment when you slow down to watch.

My unconditional love and respect and my deep gratitude are given to Michael, Chris, Ren, Melissa, Jaeden, Madison, and Serah.

Notes

The Parent Vibe—Getting your groove on
What Makes A "Good Parent"?
Diana Baumrind's work can be found in just about any introduction to psychology textbook. For a detailed look at parenting style, look up Baumrind, D. (1967) "Child care practices anteceding three patterns of preschool behavior." *Genetic Psychology Monographs, 75(1)*, 43-88.
Tips For Feeling More Control
There are a lot of versions of the "Serenity Prayer." You may be more familiar with *"God, give me the grace to accept the things that cannot be changed, the courage to change the things that can be changed, and the wisdom to know the difference."*

Attachment—Feeling like a family
The Temperament You're Born With
The work of Thomas and Chess can be found *Temperament: Theory and Practice*, by Stella Chess & Alexander Thomas (Psychology Press, 1996).
Dialing In
For more information on attunement and attachment, see *Becoming Attached*, by Robert Karen (Oxford University Press, 1998).
Never, Ever Shake A Baby
For more information on shaken baby syndrome and on ways to manage an infant's crying go to aboutshakenbaby.com.

Brain Development—The key to everything
Fetal Alcohol Syndrome
For more information on FAS, see the website of the Centers for Disease Control and Prevention at cdc.gov.
What's There To Start
My favorite site for information on brain structures and functions is Neuroscience for Kids at faculty.washington.edu/chudler/neurok.html. Updated often and written in easy to understand language, this site provides accurate information. It's a great place to start.
What Talents Did Your Child Inherit?
Thomas J. Bouchard, Jr of the University of Minnesota conducted studies of identical twins raised apart that provide evidence for the inheritability of personality traits and talents. Bouchard is quick to point out that his work doesn't mean that parenting and life experiences don't count (they do). But individuals are likely to be express interest in activities that are supported by their genetic makeup.
Preloaded Software
Mapping the Mind, by Rita Carter (University of California Press, 1998) provides a fascinating introduction to brain functions along with full-color illustrations. Again for more information on brain structures go to Neuroscience for Kids on the web from University of Washington at faculty.washington.edu/chudler/neurok.html.
Having Less
The effects of methamphetamines is described in Neuroscience for Kids. See also University Of Illinois At Urbana-Champaign, "Methamphetamine's Ruinous Effects On Children Documented In Midwest Study." ScienceDaily 15 February 2005. 9 November 2008.

Getting More
For more information on brain development and experience, see *Rethinking the Brain: New Insights into Early Development* (1997; revised October 2003), by Rima Shore, published by the Families and Work Institute and also the work of Talaris Institute at talaris.org.

Tom Edison's Mom
Information on Thomas Edison's childhood is available from the National Park Service (nps.gov).

Simple And Profound
For a variety of online resources on the effect of good relationships, real life experiences, and low stress on infant and child brain development go to the website of the National Child Care Information and Technical Assistance Center at nccic.org.

Autism: Four Things To Watch For
Much misinformation surrounds autism so it's important to use only information from reliable scientific sources, not popular media. Consult major research centers like the University of Washington to get the facts.

Brain Development Never Stops
Buy your own Morph-o-Scope at oozandoz.com. Dr. Jay Giedd is a prominent researcher in adolescent brain development at the National Institute of Mental Health at nimh.nih.gov. Look for his work on the Public Broadcasting episode *Inside the Teenage Brain* at pbs.org.

Learning To Talk—The important first step
As Natural As Breathing
See Steven Pinker's book *The Language Instinct: The New Science of Language and Mind* (Penguin, 1994) for more information on the nativist theory of language acquisition. There are competing theories of language acquisition as well, including B. F. Skinner's view that language is entirely learned through interaction with speakers and is not innate at all.

Your Role
For more information on the role of parents and conversation in children's language development see *Meaningful Differences in the Everyday Experience of Young American Children* by Todd R. Risely and Betty Hart (Paul H Brookes Publishing, 1995).

Learning Another Language
For more information on learning a first and additional languages, see the Clearinghouse on Early Education and Parenting at University of Illinois (on the web at ceep.crc.uiuc.edu).

Child Care—Who can take your place?
Going Back To Work
Sonja Michel traces the history of child care and the issues surrounding it in *Children's Interests/Mothers' Rights: The Shaping of America`s Child Care Policy* (Yale University Press, 2000).

How Early Is Too Early?
A lot of controversy surrounds infant child care and it's possible to find outraged opponents of early group care (Dr. Jay Belsky, for example) and others who dismiss opposition to early group care completely (Dr. Sandra Scarr in particular). Read carefully and get all views on this issue before you make a decision.

What It Costs
Information here is from *Parents and the High Cost of Child Care 2008 Update*, by the National Association of Child Care Resource and Referral Agencies, available at naccrra.org.
Child Care Checklist
See *Is This the Right Place for My Child ?* a booklet available at naccrra.org.
The Importance of Paying Attention
For guidance in choosing nationally accredited child care see the National Association for the Education of Young Children at naeyc.org.
Two Experts Think Outside The Box
Barbara Winter's book, *Making a Living Without a Job* (Bantam, 1993) is available at barbarawinter.com.   Kate Raidt's book *The Million Dollar Parent* is in press at this time.
Tips For Parents Of Kids Home Alone
Very few states have laws regarding the age at which children can be left alone. This only means, however, that the definition of "child neglect" is an open question, not that you may leave your child alone without fear of prosecution. If a child is left home alone and something bad happens, you can be assured that your parenting decisions will be scrutinized.
Before And After School Care
The National Afterschool Association is a resource for parents looking for quality afterschool care. See naaweb.org. The American Camp Association at acacamps.org accredits summer camps.

Brothers And Sisters—When should you have another?
Why First Borns Get All The Goodies
An interesting though slightly dated analysis of the effects of birth order is "Birth order, schooling and earnings," by Jere R. Behrman and Paul Taubman, *Journal of Labor Economics*, July 1986.
Ten Tips For Babies In Bunches
See "Twinshock: Twins Are a Hard Happiness. Issues in the Care of Multiple Birth Children" by Patricia Malmstrom, a paper presented to International Society for Twin Studies Conference, 1986. Available from ERIC document service at eric.edu.gov, publication # ED285687. See also the Clearinghouse on Early Education and Parenting at ceep.crc.uiuc.edu/poptopics/twins.html.
Sibling Rivalry
See *Family Relationships: An Evolutionary Perspective* by Catherine Salmon, Todd Kennedy Shackelford (Oxford University Press, 2008).
Step Sibs
For a discussion of the difficulty of blending families see Florida State University. "Low Grades, Bad Behavior? Siblings May Be To Blame, Study Says." ScienceDaily 9 November 2008.
The Special Needs Sib
See siblingsupport.org to find a support group for children of special needs siblings.
Small Families Are Good For The Planet
The World Without Us by by Alan Weisman (Picador, 2008).

Birds, Bees And Babies—Answering kids' questions
Where *Do* Babies Come From?
Need some help in translating sexual information into something appropriate to your child? Try reading a book. Pick something age-appropriate from the books listed at birdsandbeesandkids.com/books.
Family Legends
Keeping Family Stories Alive: Discovering and Recording the Stories and Reflections of a Lifetime by Vera Rosenbluth (Hartley & Marks, 1997) is one book to help you think about family legends. This book concentrates on gathering stories from your elders but there's no reason you can't keep a journal of your own family's happenings, starting right now. Another super resource is the work of Joe McHugh at americanfamilystories .org.
What If My Child Is Adopted?
For guidance in talking with your children about their adoption, look at adopt.org and also read *The Adoption Life Cycle: The Children and Their Families Through the Years*, by Elinor B. Rosenberg (Simon and Schuster, 1992).
Walking The Talk
Enjoy finding out about Baby Chaleco at babychaleco.com. For more information on the sexualization of children's lives in America, read *So Sexy, So Soon* by Diane Levin and Jean Kilborne (Ballantine Books, 2008).
Interview With Amy Lang
More information about Amy Lang and her advice on talking to kids about sex is at her website birdsandbeesandkids.com
Prepping For Puberty
See "First, weight; next, puberty," by Mary Beckman, *Los Angeles Times*, March 12, 2007.
What If My Child Is Gay?
This is an area of some controversy but the scientific facts are clear: homosexuality is biological, not psychological or cultural. So it's important to seek out reliable information from intelligent sources. One of the most readable explanations of the science behind homosexuality is Chandler Burr's "Homosexuality and Biology" from *The Atlantic Monthly*, March 1993 (available online at chandlerburr.com).
Sexual Decision Making
Once again, refer to Amy Lang's website at birdsandbeesandkids.com and click on Web Resources to find solid information on teen decision making.
Age-appropriate Behavior
Do read *The Hurried Child* by David Elkind (DaCapo Press, 1988/2007).

Discipline—Developing your child's self-control
Why Punishment Doesn't Work
Read Martin Henley, "Why punishment doesn't work" in the journal *Principal*, November 1997.
The Proper Way To Praise
For details on how praise can backfire, read *Punished By Rewards: The Trouble with Gold Stars, Incentive Plans, A's, Praise, and Other Bribes*, by Alfie Kohn (Mariner Books, 1999).

Offering Choices
See "Choices for Children: Why and How to Let Students Decide" by Alfie Kohn. Although Kohn is writing for teachers, his comments apply to parents just as well. This article appeared in *Phi Delta Kappan*, September 1993.

Control Issues
See "The Effect of Parental Control and Parental Care on Children's Mental Health: Does Self-Esteem Matter?" by Shirin Montazer, a paper presented at the annual meeting of the American Sociological Association, August 12, 2005.

Spanking's Wrong? Says Who?
"Spanking Kids Increases Risk Of Sexual Problems As Adults," *ScienceDaily*, retrieved August 5, 2008, from sciencedaily.com; also, "The School Bully: Does It Run In The Family?" *ScienceDaily*, retrieved August 5, 2008, from sciencedaily.com.

Never, Ever Hit A Child
Please read "Speak Softly—and Forget the Stick: Corporal Punishment and Child Physical Abuse" by Adam J. Zolotor, Adrea D. Theodore, Jen Jen Chang, Molly C. Berkoff, and Desmond K. Runyan in the *American Journal of Preventive Medicine*, October 2008.

Me, Myself And I—Your child forms an identity
Why Rebellion Is A Good Sign
Erik Erikson is the father of identity psychology. Read his most famous book, *Childhood and Society* (Vintage, 1995).

Trading In Mom And Dad
Early psychologist Harry Stack Sullivan was the first to trace the development of peer relationships in childhood and adolescence. Although some of his ideas seem old-fashioned to us now, his stages of peer relationships still hold water. A good scan of his stages is available at allpsych.com

Sleeping—Why is it such a struggle?
How Much Sleep Is Enough?
For more information, see the National Sleep Foundation at sleepfoundation.org.

Sweet Dreams And Nightmares
See Jean Piaget's, *A Child's Conception of the World* (Rowman & Littlefield, 1975) for his ideas on children's dreaming.

REM Sleep Explained
For more information on REM sleep, see the website of the federal agency National Institute of Neurological Disorders and Stroke at ninds.nih.gov.

Naps
For more about napping see the National Sleep Foundation at sleepfoundation.org.

What About Bedwetting?
For help with persistent bedwetting, see the information from the American Academy of Child and Adolescent Psychiatry at aacap.org.

Sleep Disturbances In Older Kids
See "Adolescent Sleep Disturbance and School Performance: The Confounding Variable of Socioeconomics" by James Pagel Jr., M.D in the *Journal of Clinical Sleep Medicine*, February 2007. This study reports that 60% of teens have difficulty getting to sleep at least once a week.

Food For Thought—Thinking about the food you serve
Clean Hands, Please!
The Centers for Disease Control and Prevention found that of 2874 U.S. food borne disease outbreaks, contributing factors were reported in 1435 and that poor personal hygiene was a contributing factor in *over a third* (514) of them, according to Nancy H. Bean et al., in the *Journal of Food Protection*, October 1997.
Are Foods For Kids Good For Them?
See Elliott et al. "Assessing 'fun foods': Nutritional content and analysis of supermarket foods targeted at children," in *Obesity Reviews*, 2008.
Nutrition Counts
See Paul J. Veugelers, "Children With Healthier Diets Do Better In School" from *Journal of School Health*, April 2008. In addition, the long-term effects of dairy intake is presented by Lynn Moore et al. in "Effects of Average Childhood Dairy Intake on Adolescent Bone Health," *The Journal of Pediatrics*, May, 2008.
You Can Lead A Child To Peas...
See an article by Debra Haire-Joshu, "Parents Shape Whether Their Children Learn To Eat Fruits And Vegetables" in *Preventive Medicine*, July 2008.
Not A Reward. Not A Comfort
Read "Family can shape your eating habits" by Sally Squires, *Los Angeles Times*, November 21, 2005.
Washing It Down
See David Levitsky, "Nutritional and energetic consequences of sweetened drink consumption in 6- to 13-year-old children," as reported by *Journal of Pediatrics*, June 2003.
Eating Disorders
For a downloadable pdf titled *Eating Disorders*, see National Institutes of Mental Health at nimh.nih.gov/health/publications/eating-disorders /complete-publication.
The Importance Of Family Dinners
See "Family Dinner and Diet Quality Among Older Children and Adolescents" by Matthew W. Gilman and his colleagues, *Archives of Family Medicine*, March 2000. In addition, lack of family dinnertime is linked to obesity in teens in "Frequency of Family Dinner and Adolescent Body Weight Status: Evidence from the National Longitudinal Survey of Youth, 1997" by Bisakha Sen in *Obesity*, December 2006.

Children's Bad Habits—Annoying, disgusting and embarrassing
When A Habit Isn't A Habit
See *Self-Destructive Behavior in Children and Adolescents* by Carl F. Wells (Van Rostrand Rinehold, 1981). See also the website of the American Academy of Child and Adolescent Psychiatry at aacap.org.

Friends And Enemies—Helping your child get along
Friends Over Time
See "The Development of Social Interaction from Infancy through Adolescence" by Barbara Newman, a paper presented at the Annual Meeting of the American Psychological Association, 1974. Available online at eric.ed.gov.

The Bully
Be sure to read "The School Bully: Does It Run In The Family?" a paper presented by Elizabeth Sweeney at the annual meeting of the American Sociological Association, August 5, 2008.
No Friends?
See "The Timing of Middle Childhood Peer Rejection and Friendship: Linking Early Behavior to Early Adolescent Adjustment by S. Pedersen, and colleagues in *Child Development*, Fall 2007.
Including Everyone
You can't say You can't play by Vivian Gussin Paley (Harvard University Press, 1993).

Knowing Right And Wrong—Building a conscience
Theory Of Mind
See "Theory-of-Mind Development: Retrospect and Prospect" by John Flavell, in *Merrill Palmer Quarterly*, July 2004.
Intentionality
See "Intentionality, The Heart Of Human Will," by Rollo May, *The Journal of Humanistic Psychology*, Fall 1965.
The Uh-Oh Sensor
For more from Kim Estes of P.E.A.C.E. of Mind visit her site at pomwa.org.
Staying Safe In An Unsafe World
For some clarity on how we perceive danger imperfectly and tend to exaggerate it, read *Innumeracy: Mathematical Illiteracy and Its Consequences*, by John Allen Paulos (Hill and Wang, 2001).

The Glowing Eye—Television and other media
How Bad Is Television?
Annie Dillard quote is from *The Writing Life* (Harper, 1990).
What You Watch Does Matter
For an in-depth discussion of children and media, see the entire issue "Children and Electronic Media," *Future of Children*, Spring 2008, available online at futureofchildren.org.
Video Game Ratings
Information on the Entertainment Software Rating Board is available at esrb.org.
A Fuzzy Picture
"Children and Computer Technology: Analysis and Recommendations," Margie K. Shields and Richard E. Behrman. Online at futureofchildren.org.
Kids And Online Communities
See "Social Networking Safety: A Guide for Parents," from *Future of Children* at futureofchildren.org.
The More Music, The More Musical
See Neuroscience for Kids at faculty.washington.edu/chudler/music.html
Your Kids And Their Music
See "Emotional effects of music: Production rules" by Klaus R. Scherer and Marcel R. Zentner, in *Music and emotion: Theory and research,* edited by *P. N.* Juslin & J. A. Sloboda (Oxford University Press, 2001).
Becoming A Wise Consumer
See "Talking to Kids about Advertising" from the Media Awareness Network at media-awareness.ca.

Going To School—Are we ready?
Is Preschool Necessary?
The most-referenced study of the value of preschool for low-income children comes from the High/Scope Perry Preschool Project. Information is available at highscope.org.
When To Start Kindergarten?
Darren Lubotsky and Todd Elder wrote "Starting Kindergarten Later Gives Students Only A Fleeting Edge," *Journal of Human Resources*, Fall 2008.
Elementary School And Beyond
See "The Parent's Role" at pbs.org/parents.
Why Kids Drop Out
See "High School Dropout Rates" from Child Trends DataBank at childtrendsdatabank.org. See also "Underlying Causes Of High School Dropout" from Georgia Family Connection Partnership at gafcp.org.
Off To College
See "How To Choose a College That's Right For You" by Martha O'Connell at NPR.org, February 21, 2007. See also *Almost Grown: Launching Your Child from High School to College* by P Pasick (WW Norton, 1998).

Becoming A Reader—The key step in school success
It Starts Before You Know It
See "Developmental Milestones of Early Literacy" at reachoutandread.org.
Books And Vocabulary
See Fay Shin, **"Books, Not Direct Instruction, Are the Key to Vocabulary Development"** in *Library Media Connection*, January 2004.
Conversation Is The Key
See *Meaningful Differences in the Everyday Experience of Young American Children* by Todd R. Risely and Betty Hart (Paul H Brookes Publishing, 1995).
The Power Of Story
Read "Developing Literacy Skills Through Storytelling" by Linda Fredericks, *The Resource Connection*, Spring 1997.

More Than One Way To Shine—
Helping your child find his strengths
Multiple Paths To Success
Yale neuroscientist Howard Gardner has written several books on Multiple Intelligences theory. One is *Multiple Intelligences* (Basic Books, 2006).
Life-changing Experiences
The story of Yehudi Menuhin is recounted by Howard Gardner in his *Multiple Intelligences* (Basic Books, 2006).
How Scheduled Is Over-Scheduled?
See also David Elkind's *The Hurried Child* (Da Capo Press, 2006).
Should Your Teen Get A Job?
Take a look at "Teen at Work: The Burden of a Double Shift on Daily Activities," by Liliane Reis Teixeira and her colleagues, in *Chronobiology International*, December 2004.

Disruptions And Detours—Helping children cope with change
Moving Away
A clear discussion of the impact of homelessness is in *There's No Place Like Home*, edited by Anna Lou Dehavenon (Bergin and Garvey, 1999).

Separation And Divorce
Read "Children And Divorce," from the American Academy of Child and Adolescent Psychiatry, at aacap.org.
New Family Members
See *Raising Children in Blended Families: Helpful Insights, Expert Opinions, and True Stories* by Maxine Marsolini (Kregel, 2006).
Illness And Injury
See *How to Help Children Through a Parent's Serious Illness* by Kathleen McCue (St. Martin's Griffen, 1996).
Death
For a book to read with children, see *Why Do People Die?: Helping Your Child Understand with Love and Illustrations* by Cynthia MacGregor (Citadel, 1999). Also, *Talking with Children and Young People About Death and Dying: A Resource* by Mary Turner (Jessica Kingsley, 2006).
Do Things Come In Threes?
See "Children's Coping Assistance: How Parents, Teachers, and Friends Help Children Cope After a Natural Disaster" by Mitchell J. Prinstein and his colleagues, in the *Journal of Clinical Child & Adolescent Psychology*, February 1996.

Making It All Better—What to do if you've screwed up
To Err Is Human
See "What We Regret Most ... and Why" by Neal J. Roese and Amy Summerville, *Personality and Social Psychology Bulletin*, September 2005.
Accepting The Present As It Is
See *On Becoming a Person* by Carl Rogers (Mariner Books, 1995).
Every Day Is A New Opportunity
One resource is *Breaking Free, Starting Over: Parenting in the Aftermath of Family Violence* by Christina M. Dalpiaz (Greenwood Publishing Group, 2004).

Leaving Footsteps To Follow—Becoming a family leader
Be Remembered As A Scaffold
Although the idea of scaffolded instruction is based on Vygotsky's work, he never used that term himself. The term is attributed instead to American psychologist Jerome Bruner, writing in the 1950s.
Be Remembered As A Refuge
"The Death of the Hired Man," in *North of Boston*, by Robert Frost (Henry Holt and Company, 1915).
Be Remembered As Unconditional
See *On Becoming a Person* by Carl Rogers (Mariner Books, 1995).

My Message To You

Family is important to me. I come from a long line of preachers and teachers and hard-scrabble farmers in tough times. My paternal grandfather emigrated from Sweden at the turn of the last century. My maternal grandmother worked as a cook in a logging camp in northern Minnesota. They handed down to my generation values of hard work, supportive relationships, and optimism. In this guide, I'm handing those on to you.

I taught school in an inner city neighborhood for many years and my husband and I raised two fine sons. I became a single parent and struggled to keep things together. I earned a doctoral degree and became a college professor. At every step along the way the importance of family and the role of parents became more and more clear to me. I finally gave up my university position to devote my time to you. To you and your family.

Nothing is more important than this. Nothing is more important than your success as a parent. Parenting is where the development of human potential begins. It is the cornerstone of national productivity, artistic expression, technological innovation, and spiritual growth. Every good thing that happens between us happens first at home.

So I am at your service. Please call me, ask me to drop by to talk with you, have me in to talk with your employees, your associates and your friends. Pass this book along to someone whom I should get to know. Join in the conversation on my website at parentingafieldguide.com. What you're doing is important work and I'm here to help. Together we can achieve for your family and for the world every good thing.

Work With Dr. Anderson

"Every good thing that happens between us happens first at home." Engaging Dr. Anderson's wisdom and expertise is a step in making good things happen in your family, your organization, and in the wider world we all share.

Patricia Nan Anderson is available to speak at your conference, convention or business summit on issues of leadership and human potential. She can provide a keynote address, interactive workshop or personal consultation for the benefit of your employees, members or constituents. She is ready to serve on your expert panel, be a member of your advisory team, or contribute to your strategic planning efforts. She is here to help you with your personal child rearing challenges.

Whatever the interest of your organization or family focus, the development of children and youth is a central concern to its future and the future of the nation. Dr. Anderson's understanding of developmental psychology, motivation and learning, and her years of experience as an educator, motivational speaker, parent and consultant, make her uniquely capable to contribute to that future.

Each engagement is tailored to your needs. Whether you are the leader of a parent group, a small business coordinator, a meeting planner, CEO of a major corporation, or the mom down the street, Dr. Anderson stands ready to assist you in developing your parenting skills or enhancing your support of children and families. For more details, please visit her website at parentingafieldguide.com.

With Dr. Anderson's guidance, you can bring out the best in the children in your care. Together, you and she can achieve great things.

Index